Digitized Product Management

A Guide to Reinventing Your Business Through Digitalization

by Agathe Daae-Qvale

PUBLISHED BY TINKERBLUE AS

Digitized Product Management

A Guide to Reinventing Your Business Through Digitalization

by

Agathe Daae-Qvale

Typesetting and cover design: Teena Clipston
Cover photo credit: Yuyeung Lau / Unsplash
Back cover photo credit: Aideal Hwa / Unsplash
Vector diagram credits: Vecteezy.com & Flaticon.com

Glossary generated by Chat GPT. OpenAI sharing policy:
https://openai.com/policies/sharing-publication-policy

For information visit: https://tinkerblue.com

Paperback ISBN: 9798398991529

"When you come to the end of all the light you know, and it's time to step into the darkness of the unknown, faith is knowing that one of two things shall happen: either you will be given something solid to stand on or you will be taught to fly."

Edward Teller

CONTENTS

DIAGRAMS

PART 1

ON INNOVATION

INTRODUCTION

The room fell silent, as I had just finished a rather long row of arguments. I had explained how my client's production line could benefit from the introduction of AI use cases. In this situation, use cases referring to specific situations in which a technology product or service could be applied. This was not the first time my enthusiasm for tech had rendered my listeners slightly perplexed. The CEO was slowly twisting a pen in front of him with two hands while he looked at me from above his glasses. "You certainly have some interesting ideas," he countered after a short silence.

The COO next to him stared into his PC. He explained to me that many of the changes I had proposed were not yet possible. Their digital transformation plan had already been decided. Looking across the room, I observed quizzical looks. These were the people I sought to demonstrate the extreme range of benefits—specific to their needs, production lines, and more—of engaging in a digital transformation. I could see it and their company's future. I wanted them to reach a shared understanding in order to gain clear and measurable results.

However, the time they allotted me was all-too-brief. An hour of dialogue was over, with strategies and methods still on the edge of my tongue. They were packing up and pushing back from the table, rushing out of the room. I left the room reassured that some deemed my advisory services worthwhile and interesting, though perhaps not the ones making the decisions. I was dumbfounded by the blank stares I had received. I realized, once more, that salient parts of my consultation had not reached its most important audience. My core advice would likely not be integrated.

I suspected that all the discussions would be discounted, all my reports would be stuck in a drawer, and all their "yes, but" responses during my consulting term would keep them stuck with minimal change to prepare them for the digital shifts no individual or company can afford to ignore. Chances were that the list of suggested changes to their large IT landscape, if not implemented, would result in nothing more than loose ends. A far cry from the vision of the end game I saw possible for their company.

The best-case scenario would leave some feeble transformation initiatives, while not much else would happen as a consequence of my work after I left the client.

Now things are different.

After years of wondering how to be more effective, I dedicated myself to the search for an approach that could clarify the path needed for success in digital transformation.

My intention in sharing this meeting experience is to show what happened way too often in my early consulting career and as a cautionary tale to anyone engaging in management consulting in tech. At times, in the closing of a short-term IT strategy engagement, a shared understanding of what a digital transformation should encompass was not in place. It felt like there was a lack of engagement from the top management, which imitated a closing immediately after I began. In my search to achieve the desired impact, I discovered methods to carve out a new space where I could portray the greater picture. I developed the means to portray a rich backdrop against which this scene of digital opportunity could play out.

There is huge potential for open-ended discussions in the space of the current digital transformation. I now have more space to explore the power behind the advice I have shared over the last two decades. Awakening basic curiosity is the key to opening a two-way field of understanding of not only what needs to be done but also why it needs to be done.

TRANSFORMATIONAL ENIGMAS

Some encompassing conundrums have remained the same both before and after so many of the transformation projects we witness. The more recent the project, the more crucial and pointed the challenges seem to be. Here are some of the most important fast-growing challenges:

- We are pushing a wall of digitalization in front of us and the organization. This makes it understandable why it is hard to prioritize activities. Especially for the ones on the front lines who need to make time-sensitive decisions.
- A need to feel secure compels me, my peers, and clients to digitalize reactively as we all try to follow market developments. This results in the organization looking backwards and sometimes sideways, while we cannot clearly see enough future value as a consequence of our digital choices.
- This is the time to develop a new vision and way of tracking which technologies will change our products' market conditions in the near future. The market used to take years to change, then for some time it took months, and now I see important milestones in global development happening only weeks apart.
- Digital skills and understanding of important drivers must be as fluid as the disappearing borders of technological advances, or they risk becoming outdated in an ever-faster-moving world.
- The world around us is accelerating through new technologies in directions that are hard to understand and even harder to follow. It is my role to assist in moving from confusion to proactivity.

These are the core enigmas I explore in this book. I want you, the reader, to better understand the drivers behind the raging developments in the world today. When you have finished reading, I want you to be better prepared for the digital transformation you're already a central part of. I want you to be proactive in your digital and digitized product management, not only reactive.

PEOPLE AND TECHNOLOGY

The answer to the question of why my clients avoid the digital transformation or reduce it to a shadow of what it could be is that we are all human. We are all different. I can sympathize with everyone who chooses or is forced to deal with the various daily challenges of business operations rather than spending time contemplating a future that is uncertain at best.

I believe I am witnessing a fair share of reactive leadership where proactive leadership would be far more profitable in the long term.

At the same time, I need to be aware of displaying any hint of arrogance by assuming I know better than my clients, seemingly sabotaging any forward movement. Am I only seeking a shared understanding of how I see the world, or am I seeking a constructive dialogue on the client's terms? Could I possibly be the only one in the room that has the luxury of spending so much time working on challenges that, for many, belong in a far-fetched future? The impression sinks in that many around me believe they would be happier if I could only stop bringing up so many questions to which they don't have strong answers.

I will keep trying to communicate to people around me what the world looks like through my eyes, both when I feel lonely in doing so and when others are skeptical as to what I have to say. At times, there is an imminent gloom over what new technologies have to offer. The underlying conflicted emotions of excitement and fear will dictate how human individuals let go or rigidly hang on to control.

There is no way I can stop talking about this very expression of what humanity is capable of creating because, as much as tech can be seen as complicated, it also brings out so much joy and opportunity.

To me, tech brings out hope for what we can achieve as humans and what we may be capable of bringing into the world. In parallel, with tech manifesting how humanity is unfolding in the best of ways, there are also words of caution that I consider vital. So much so that it pains me if they go unsaid.

To me, 'technology' is such a broad term that it is of no use to differentiate it from human creation. For the sake of context, I like to compare it to concepts and items like firearms, cars, or the internet. Human history has rarely seen such strong tools before these emerged and quickly became common across the planet. The development of tech is currently accelerating exponentially. Mass improvements in both numbers and scale are unprecedented, so there is nothing that can dampen my curiosity as to where this will end. I like to believe it will all end well. The expression of ourselves as humans is always reflected in our innovations, for good and for bad. In my world, the tool at hand is not to be feared, while the intention behind its use should be. I believe that the application of technology is what will guide us towards our shared future. I see no way to avoid the shared destination that technology will bring us, no matter how easy it is to avoid the harder questions in our daily lives.

How will tech influence our near and far future? What will tech bring to the children and grandchildren of people alive today? For me, it is impossible to avoid those questions. I will make an attempt to explain what I believe this current time holds in terms of human application of tech, and how we can make step-by-step innovation work for our benefit. New global powers can be harnessed and controlled as much as any old power in history. Today's tech innovation has reached a point where I like to compare the use cases of today to standing on the shoulders of giants. The giant of product management consists of older tech and use cases mostly developed over the last decades. Digital information in the form of data is forming a shoulder that innovative use cases can stand on today. Digital information connectivity is forming the other shoulder. I believe innovation has not been so powerful, disruptive, and effective for us humans for a long time, perhaps not since the combustion engine was invented or the large-scale introduction of the electricity grid.

As humans, we can choose to work with the tech being introduced in our time, ignore it, or straight out work against it. I prefer to work with it and make it work for me and for others. That is why I am driven to engage with people and reduce the quizzical looks in meeting rooms. I continue to convey my vantage point on the opportunities laid out in front of us all. I do so not because I think I am more right in my observations than anyone else, but because I think the discussion on innovative tech choices for those who make them is crucial. These choices will clear the way to claiming business opportunities, dealing with internal and external threats, and making meaningful, constructive choices leading to successful product management.

As I discuss digitalization and digitization throughout this book, I would like to give a thankful nod to Hassaim Abdul Malak and his blog, *The ECM Consultant*[1]. He succinctly describes the distinction between the two as follows: "Digitization is the process of transforming information from a physical format to a digital version, while digitalization is the practice of utilizing technology to enhance corporate processes."

The evolution of tech is really not that hard to understand; only the

---

1   https://theecmconsultant.com/digitization-vs-digitalization/

increasing pace is new to us. Innovative tech needs relevant context to be understood properly and applied efficiently. Artificial intelligence (AI), big data, the Internet of Things (IoT) and machine learning (ML) may seem like daunting concepts to work with. This perception changes when it shows that they are merely tools enabling old problems to be resolved in new ways.

The terms AI and ML can be confusing, but they have different meanings. ML, part of AI, employs computer systems that are able to learn by analyzing data to discern patterns. AI refers to computer-based technology that imitates natural or human intelligence by being able to process large volumes of data, in order to accomplish a goal.

The problems AI and ML solve often turn out to be as old as rock, and it is the approach to innovation itself that creates the arena where new tech solutions emerge. I have gained valuable insights working with emerging technologies manifested through innovative use cases. My hope is to engage the reader. I want engaging and informed conversations to take place both inside and outside boardrooms.

In more than 20 years of working with technology, people, and processes, I have come across numerous approaches towards digitalization leading to innovation. Some have without a doubt been more valuable and efficient than others, while none of them have been complete. I have read books, papers, articles, and invested in topical training sessions, and yet I have found every method, framework, and theory I have come across lacking and/or often product or business specific. In addition, the approach to innovation is often dependent on the situation, the experience of the leadership involved, and the specific market to be addressed. I have become increasingly aware of a more wholesome approach to innovation that can be applied universally, independent of product, type of business, or market area.

In my work, I have been involved in various change projects, always trying to introduce technologies that leverage people and processes. Asking people to change, without exception, has always been the greatest challenge in every case in which I have worked. Even when technology has seemingly been the culprit, it has turned out in the end, every time, that the problem at its core has been human nature—the resistance to real change. The easiest thing to change has always been the tech part. Despite its increased complexity, tech is always rather black and white. Processes can be discussed back and forth, and they can always be described in some way on a piece of paper. People often struggle with change.

Sometimes change projects take the seemingly easy approach of replacing people within an organization, such as assigning new titles and new roles. This change of perspective is often an attempt to make change easier by changing the understanding of human beings and their place with technology and processes by labeling people differently. You may notice how change-makers talk about organizations rather than looking at and searching for relevant key aspects in individuals.

Still, when applying changes to organizations by describing new roles and formulating new job profiles and skills, one still must deal with actual people. Managers and leaders will need to adapt and innovate in their communication. Each individual has the wisdom to contribute, and the new information must be understood and integrated for successful long-term coalescing.

Various people in most organizations usually have a wide array of roles. They are strategists, architects, planners, developers, technicians, end-users, operators, and any person who will be involved in even thinking about new tech. The organization consists of individuals and teams who will plan for new technology, develop it, implement it and in many cases, eventually use it.

It can be challenging to separate personal bias and subjectivity from the processes of change and innovation. For many, there is no difference between the two. It is all new and probably feels a bit unknown to the person it affects. Still, innovation stands apart from change because it breaks new ground and includes changes that are not yet commonly made. After all, innovation is the result of new ideas that few or none have actualized before. Often, a novel idea has been commonly shared for some time but has not yet been realized or applied.

Fresh ideas are often difficult to incorporate. Already at this point, the reasons why innovation is challenging start to differentiate from the challenges of change. When defining the challenges of innovation, the reasons immediately seem to split in every direction. Some examples could be because of a lack of known suitable materials for a product, because of a lack of knowledge as to how a product should be made, or simply because the process of achieving the new and unexplored terrain is known but too expensive to realize. On the other hand, the idea could be great, but an important stakeholder may not believe the market needs an augmented product as there are existing alternatives in the market.

The list of challenges to innovation is long. The shared trait is the human reluctance to shift towards the unknown, and there are numerous additional complications. To manifest the unknown is far more challenging than to manifest what is partly understood. Any imagined obstacle could put a creative and innovative process on hold or prevent the augmentation of a production process from being realized. An improvement of an existing process may be easier for many to tolerate than the exchange or elimination of an entire process. The improvement of processes introduces a smaller scale of human change than the replacement and disruption of processes. In this way, the degree of innovation can be seen as provoking various levels of human resistance to change. The greater the change, the stronger the human resistance, generally speaking.

Dance in the head of the creator to see the innovative ideas, and there you will find the earliest known point of every invention. From there on, it all depends on good communication, good documentation, and good execution from the idea to the product, service, or delivery. As soon as the idea is articulated in any way, whether spoken or written, it will be subject to scrutiny, questioning, and criticism from others. Often, the critical person is in a state of resistance. Resistance to innovation is harnessed by powerfully conveying what innovation actually is and why it is needed. There is a lot of randomness in the critique of innovation, similar to how fear of the unknown lies deep inside most of us. The bigger the shift required by the new idea from the status quo, the greater the resistance will be among some people, but not all. So, to get the backdrop of innovation in place, let's take a brief look at the psychology of change and how it is likely to affect the innovative process.

PSYCHOLOGY OF CHANGE
"The bad news is you're falling through the air, nothing to hang on to, no parachute. The good news is there's no ground." - Chogyam Trungpa

Marketing people have known this for ages, as have psychologists and neuroscientists, and it really is basic. Some people are eager to take risks, while others are searching for security in every situation they are in. Think of an example of almost any couple you know. One person wants to do a home rebuilding project, while the other is holding back for one or more reasons. One reason could be to save money. Another could be that he or she likes the home the way it is or that the newly offered change does not provide enough benefits to warrant going through the change. This is often the difference between driving change and resisting it. One of the two will often accept and take more risks than the other. We may already understand this from how we look at the world around us, or we may have learned about the psychology of change in school or through higher education. Still, we tend to get into new subjective discussions on whether the change or innovative idea is viable or worth the price almost every time we come across one. When it comes to how we all feel about change, it usually makes no difference if the change is happening in our private lives or in our work sphere in the form of the introduction of new tech. Resistance to change is deeply ingrained in most of us, whether we actively look for it or resist it. There is plenty of material describing the psychology of change. For anyone who wants to indulge in the topic of human change, which is vast, one option would be to study the books of Robert Kegan[2]. Two relevant examples of books he has written or strongly contributed to are *Immunity to Change* and *An Everyone Culture*.

A LOOK AT INNOVATORS

We have all heard of people like Elon Musk, Steve Jobs, or Thomas Edison. We know them as innovation pioneers who have invented great solutions or products to solve big problems. These are representatives who many people today admire and look to when it comes to driving the world forward. Let me introduce you to other innovators I admire. A father and son from my small hometown are building a cabin together. They keep running up against practical obstacles, particularly when building stairs. Together, they find joy in resolving small practical challenges together throughout the building process. Personally, I don't think this kind of low-key innovation is any less great than the more famous kind capable of putting electric cars into orbit around Earth. Musk's marketing activities may be more spectacular. However, the quiet, everyday process of finding solutions to problems happening daily in so many homes is perhaps at least as important in driving the world forward.

So what needs to be in place for innovation to happen? Clearly, very few of us are born as famous entrepreneurs or driven home improvers. Can the way we frame innovation itself be a challenge? If we frame innovation too narrowly, we may miss out on big value, and if we define it too widely, the energy of innovation may fall flat as we lose focus. How can one know

---

2   https://en.wikipedia.org/wikiwiki/Robert_Kegan#An_Everyone_Culture

that a specific piece of innovation will hit the sweet spot and deliver real value? One could study a lot of great ideas that never quite got realized or solutions that ended up too far from the problems they were originally intended to resolve. A far better option is to look at successful innovations that were, or weren't, planned as innovations in the first place. Let's face it: sometimes innovations like homemade glue come from a failed baking project, or a simple painkiller turns out to be an efficient heart medication (aspirin in this case).

There are many forms and stages of innovation, and there are many ways to describe such variations. Anything from disruptive innovations like fire, electricity, and the internet, which have changed so many lives, to continuous improvements that we hardly notice even when they happen right in front of our eyes—the star-shaped hole in the aluminum tube of mayonnaise, new patterns on car tires, and the elimination of patient queues in hospitals for routine operations as surgeons use kick bikes between hospital buildings to spend more minutes in surgery than between—these are all examples of less noticeable improvements that happen continuously around us every day. We may notice that accumulated change has happened over the course of many years, while incremental steps and innovations are often just small enough that we don't pay much attention. Directional, consecutive, smaller changes may feel less disruptive in our lifetimes, but really, it is only the scale of the timeline that makes a difference. What we humans often perceive as disruptive are large leaps of innovation or change in a relatively short time span, while equally large changes drawn out over time may feel less dramatic and disruptive in our lives. Many organizations and businesses work with continuous improvement in the long term as a way to optimize internal processes or improve an established product. In this way, they try to avoid stagnation and continuously strive for improvement in areas that matter. It is often when other organizations and markets come up with game-changing innovations in a shorter period of time that we see them as disruptive. Electric cars have disrupted the human mobility market in a relatively short amount of time. If the introduction of electric solutions in a car, including the engine, had happened partially over a hundred years, it would likely have felt less disruptive and more like a natural development of both product, market, and customer behavior. Hybrid cars with both combustion and electric motors became mainstream after the electric car disrupted the market for petrol- and diesel-driven cars. If the shift to electric cars had been slower, we may have seen that hybrid cars would have been a natural development of the product, but because of the relatively short time span of the market shift and the perceived disruption of petrol-driven engines, we may now look at hybrid cars as a reaction to the market disruption by electric cars. Time sure heals wounds, even in the markets.

The majority of projects and jobs I have delivered have dealt with continuous improvement. In between, there were projects and jobs dealing with disruptive technologies. Still, I have probably worked on far more disruptive technologies and markets than most in my field, as I have actively searched for disruptive market situations to get involved in. I have taken career risks and pay cuts exceeding 60% to get into the company cultures and business areas where I expected disruption to happen. Sometimes the role has been secondary to me, as long as I could get close enough to where the magic of innovation and change would happen. Honestly, I have also learned to scrutinize my future boss and leadership before accepting almost any role, as their mentality and attitude would rule my day-to-day life, hence being a huge success factor for my own success. If my boss will not innovate and disrupt, then it becomes exceedingly hard for me to do so. Sometimes my efforts got rewarded, and a few times I missed that exhilarating ride of disruptive innovation. It often came down to the company culture and, more precisely, the nine dimensions described in "Part 3" of this book, whether the development of exciting new products and services would fly or not.

A few times over the years, I have worked with companies dealing with internal causes of fraud or theft. In every single case, the organization had done everything within its power to correct the situation. I suppose I would not have been hired for the job to reestablish internal operations with sufficient process quality controls and transparency if that were not the case in the first place. Internal and external reestablishment of trust towards the organization and business have been the first priorities for all involved during these projects. When it comes to disruption, I rate these projects and jobs very highly. I have witnessed the eagerness to not be at fault and to be as much a driver for change as any high aspirations concerning innovation and disruption. In other words, decisions are often defensive and fear-driven. Corrective intention is just as important as the intention to grow and disrupt markets when it comes to innovation.

It is worth reflecting on the human drivers of change, including innovation and disruption of any kind. These drivers are rooted in our emotions on individual, group, and cultural levels. In western culture, we tend to focus on what we want as individuals, strive to achieve this image, and often share it as a mirage with others as we create businesses and organizations to make our visions a reality. To better understand the human drivers for change and innovation, I believe it is worthwhile to explore our human sides as well and not only focus on technology. After all, most technologies and innovations will only become as good as we are, unless we strike pure luck.

Many innovations, or inventions, we see around us today are a result of the application of the empirical method. During the Renaissance, 500 years ago, this method was introduced as a reliable way to harness and enhance the process of innovation. The result today is that research facilities and universities alike have relied on empirical methods for 500 years and still do to establish new truths. In parallel, one can observe that many innovators are coming up with ideas precisely because they are setting established processes and truths aside. Without the ability to 'think outside the box' and work outside established processes, new ideas and concepts are difficult to conceive and even harder to realize. The empirical method is often identified as the scientific method, which is the golden standard of methodology driving the evolution of science globally today. As a method based on principles, it has proven to stand the test of time without being outdated.

Still, in my view, it could prove useful to look beyond the empirical method and take a broader look at innovation. I refer to the instinctual "thinking outside the box". A new perspective can harness fresh vantage points from which ideas can be conceived and realized into new concepts. This is the same as asking where the hypothesis originates while freeing the mind from any previous process. I am not only referring to the space between the process-oriented scientist who drives innovation by strict method and the eccentric inventor who denies as much process as possible in the quest to find solutions to known problems. I am looking toward a wider and more universal approach to innovation. An approach that many can work with and is driven by principles. An approach that does not make people find themselves in a limiting environment for any practical reason. It is by no means a complete map of how innovation should work. It is rather a proposal as to how innovation could work across many disciplines and cultures when certain principles and areas of innovation challenges are observed.

This book proposes a tangible map forward towards innovation and the development of use cases based on principles in such a way that a balance between excess process focus and pure randomness may be found. Any innovation needs to be grounded enough in reality while striving for enough lightness of touch to make an agile approach work efficiently.

HOW TO WORK WITH INNOVATION

It is necessary to move beyond frameworks like empirical methods and more recently described methods, such as 'Open Space Technology[3]' where ideas are harvested and dealt with in very efficient ways. If you have not heard about this method and are interested in the collaborative creation process, you may look up the author Harrison Owen and his book *Open Space Technology: A User's Guide*. The book explores a sound recipe for how creative workshops and problem-solving may be run and is founded on the basic principles of human group collaboration before workshops of various kinds were named workshops.

There are several astoundingly good methods for innovation, and yet, I do miss an articulated set of principles, or even rules, that apply to them all across history and culture. I prefer to work with a set of principles that apply to how we, as humans and organizations, work with ideas that we come up with ourselves or come across that we would like to work with and realize. When we leave judgment of the origin of an idea behind, we are getting somewhere. Professionally trained product concept incubators in corporate departments are often opposed to informal artistic innovation, and vice versa.

For sure, there are innovation departments within corporate companies across the world that have brilliant minds employed and that create more working ideas than most of us would ever manage to come up with in a lifetime. Without taking an informal and often more random process of innovation into account, we would miss out on the greatest ideas surfacing daily in our world. It may be hard to see for some, but I would claim that the ingenuity of artistic works and musical oeuvres does not have to depend on the vantage point or opinion of the artist or composer who created them. The unique and useful application of anything new depends on how it is realized, put into this world, and perceived by others. It is not the origin of a tool that matters the most; it is how it is planned for, developed, implemented, and used that makes all the difference. The philosophical question of whether a light exists if nobody sees it can be interpreted as

---

3   https://en.wikipedia.org/wiki/Open_Space_Technology

if nobody observes or understands a piece of innovation: can the new concept truly be innovative, or is it only a random event for the world?

So why is it so hard to make something really innovative? I believe the bottom-line answer is that it is equally hard to imagine something new and different outside the box as it is to plan for it, develop it, and make it work universally. Try to explain what a spaceship is to someone who has never heard of the concept or seen one. This means that anything new needs to be communicated, understood, and agreed upon between several people before any efficient work can start turning the innovative idea into reality and value. Then one may discover that new tools are needed to materialize this innovation, perhaps even new methods and processes as well. In the end, it is not unusual to wonder if new heads are needed, particularly if the theory and practice of human change require more attention. The path to innovation is often based on trying and failing. It takes way more time than expected to convey and articulate it appropriately so that others may understand it. More often than not, entirely new concepts are abandoned due to a lack of common direction and shared understanding across heads, departments, and markets for new concepts solving old problems.

Matt Asay, a seasoned tech columnist, wrote the following about big data projects back in 2017:

A year ago, Gartner estimated that 60% of big data projects fail. As bad as that sounds, the reality is actually worse. According to Gartner analyst Nick Heudecker this week, Gartner was "too conservative" with its 60% estimate. The real failure rate? "[C]loser to 85 percent." In other words, abandon hope all ye who enter here, especially because "[T]he problem isn't technology," Heudecker said. It's you.[4]

What can be done with challenges to innovation, often not wholly anticipated by leadership or participants from the start? First, I believe the idea of having one method of innovation fit all new concepts is an illusion in itself. There is no such thing. Before imagining something entirely new, there may be an infinite number of ways to achieve it. That is why an inside-out approach is needed, one that is independent of niche, vertical, leadership personality, market, and area of business. A way that is based on principles, in the same way that other approaches have stood strong during the test of time, like the empirical

---

4   https://www.techrepublic.com/article/85-of-big-data-projects-fail-but-your-developers-can-help-yours-succeed/

method or the method that appears in *Open Space Technology.*

In the context of this book, innovation will move beyond the traditional change triangle of people, process, and technology. Innovation is about more than connecting the organization, that is to say, its people, with technology and processes in new ways. It is about how we, as human beings, work with new ideas that confront existing ways of being that currently matter.

PART 2

CONTEXT OF USE CASE DEVELOPMENT

PROXIMITY TO CORE PRODUCT

A surprising number of us tend to focus on what is less important during our workday. It has been claimed that many of us spend more time on non-critical matters during work hours than on being productive. This is not a matter of spending time reading news online when we should have spent time writing that product sheet. It is more a matter of asking yourself and your organization how many hours should be spent working on the product sheet in place of the hours spent directly with or on the specific product. I believe the hours spent working on a product sheet may be reduced significantly, while the hours spent on the product should be maximized.

There are clearly different types of companies and organizations according to markets and domains, as well as in the form of first-, second-, and third-generation companies. First-generation companies, typically young startups, need to focus entirely on the development of their products and sales functions. Simultaneously, they work extremely efficiently to not fold within the first few months or years of existence.

Second-generation companies and organizations usually start to feel a bit more confident and often focus on consolidating their operations, fleshing out the number of employees as they focus on building supportive functions. Besides HR, finance, and service management, they also need to focus on the important sales and product development tasks they started with initially.

Third-generation companies are mostly settled, old, and large organizations. They may, or may not, be in danger of becoming complacent about their market shares as they trust their client base and often have a brand that is well-known in the marketplace. Third-generation companies may perceive themselves as successful actors in the market. They often feel the need to focus on keeping their market share with existing products rather than innovating new solutions for an ever-changing market. Historically, some markets are more static than others; for instance, could the private lawn mower market be considered more static than the ever-changing gaming market?

However, in the last few years, the status quo of many static markets has been changed by a phase of disruption. For instance, where the lawnmower with a combustion engine has been a common sight across the world for decades, electric lawnmowers with built-in GPS and ML functionality are becoming increasingly common. Updated models of smart lawn mowers as well as updates of their software may be launched as frequently as any gaming engine online. We talk about counting months, not years. Such a shift forces any company to work differently in many ways at multiple levels. Production companies are forced to incorporate agility in place of working with static long-term plans. They are also forced to rethink their organizational functions and where to put their focus efficiently.

In the book *ReWork: Change the Way You Work Forever*[5] , the authors Jason Fried and David Heinemeier Hansson claim that planning is guessing. Even if their book focuses largely on the shifting landscape of startups, their observations are just as valid for any generation of company or organization. Agile and light approaches are needed for globally shifting markets as tech innovation forces companies and organizations to speed up their pace of innovation, internally and externally. The reality of global markets has shifted into higher gears. New and unknown territories need to be dealt with, perhaps for every part of an organization.

In this fast-paced world, companies need to pay increasing attention to shifting markets as well as the changing demands of their internal operations. Spending energy and time on internal supportive functions is

---

5   https://www.amazon.de/-/en/David-Heinemeier-Hansson/dp/0091929784/

increasingly becoming a stretched item on the list of costs. As the landscape of competitors shifts faster and faster, knowing what really matters in the organization becomes increasingly important. Not only for the sake of cost-saving but because it is more important than ever to understand what the core deliverables are for the organization. Chasing new markets is increasingly vital. So is understanding exactly where to focus within core value chains, core services, and core products to be able to succeed in the shifting market landscape.

SHIFT IN STRATEGIC DIVERSIFICATION

It is worthwhile to pay good attention to the differentiation between market strategy and product development. Since the introduction of Michael Porter's generic strategies[6] in the 1980s, the strategic outlook for most global conglomerates has shifted and become more nuanced. Where many conglomerates used to diversify their product portfolio to avoid the risks of changing markets, large companies have increasingly either specialized their product(s) to differentiate themselves in the market or chosen a low-cost position for their product(s) to ensure their market share. One of the two has been the well-trodden way to strategic market advantage for many over the last 40 years. The idea of diversifying risks has simultaneously been lifted to the ownership level of conglomerates and large corporations. Diversifying investments in large companies have, to some extent, replaced diversifying product portfolios on a company-conglomerate level.

In parallel, organizations developing products and services have increasingly been funneled into standardization with the application of common frameworks for their internal operations. Where companies used to find their own, unique solutions to problems, larger system applications have been streamlining internal operations and developments for more than a generation.

In times past, a certain focus used to be on the product, while today company ownership matters more than ever. This has forced the CEO to increasingly orient towards the owners of the company, while the COO, CTO, and the Product Manager have been increasingly oriented towards efficiency and standardization. The value chains of the CEO have become narrower and more specialized, while the value chains of top operational management in the form of the COO and CTO have become wider, much

---

6   https://www.amazon.com/Competition-Updated-Expanded-Michael-Porter/dp/142212696X

like a motorway has higher capacity and faster movement than the narrow track to a mountain peak the CEO is forced to follow.

This matters because the vision, which forms the foundation of every goal and strategy of the company, is increasingly anchored in the ownership of the company, often through large private investment portfolios. At the same time, the goals, strategy, and KPIs are dictating the operational level of the company, including product development.

In this book, I share the perspective of innovation applied in product development more than the perspective of the CEO dealing with the vision of the company's ownership. Some may say that innovation belongs where the vision is, while I work with the concept that a vision, and hence innovation, can be held on just about any level and place imaginable. For the purpose of clarity and context, I mostly focus on the product level, where, for instance, patents are developed.

IMPORTANCE OF MARKET PROCESS

A colleague of mine working for a global cosmetics firm entrusted me with the information that the company spent about 70% of almost every new product budget on various forms of marketing costs. Often, no more than 10% of the investment went directly into the core product's development. The focus was all on how the product would sell at a given volume and take a given share of the market. It was not the novelty of the product itself that mattered most.

Sure, a moisturizer is a proven product, and the list of new ingredients in this specific product matters, but it is still how it is put on the market that matters most. If it does not sell, then there could be no more new moisturizers launched in the future. In this case, the product innovation factor matters less than the innovation of the marketing campaign because market share is more important. For this line of products, innovation will be focused heavily on marketing strategies and perhaps on business models, while less on the product itself.

This shift of innovation focus from product to market is an important point that seems to slide into the shadows for various businesses and organizations creating new products. Many tech startups could have been saved if they had focused as much on sales and marketing as they did on product development. Having the world's best product does not help much if not enough customers are aware of its existence. By not paying attention to markets and the related business drivers, many companies focus on their product development only to discover that the product they love so much themselves is not loved as much by people outside the company.

The practical reason for failure on a tactical level, in this case, could be a lack of good communication of what the product actually is and does. It could be a failed focus on understanding how the customer values the new product, or there is no need for this specific product in the market. If we pivot that last reason around, it could easily be that the market needs to be created for the new product. Consumers cannot know the new and unknown unless they are appropriately informed. This last observation is often the end-of-narrative conundrum for a lot of tech innovators. They have great innovations lined up for scaling, but they are not well seasoned in the fields of sales and marketing.

In the case of the new product launch for the global cosmetic firm mentioned above, the cosmetic firm has understood that the innovative factor of the product is the marketing campaign, not the moisturizer or core product itself. The end consumer perceives the main product to be the moisturizer because that is what the end-user puts money down to purchase. The end consumer does not need to know that the most important product development for the cosmetic company is an innovative marketing campaign. After all, consumer markets are usually ruled by emotions, and the perceived need for a specific product is what makes the sale, not the logic behind the technicalities of the core product itself.

This is a bit of a mind-twister for many outside the commercial, product development, and marketing departments of this world. It can be tempting for consumers to articulate a personal defense if someone suggests they are easily 'tricked' or tempted into buying consumer goods by clever marketing campaigns. What is the quality of our necessities? What makes us pick one product over another? These questions can soon turn into a labyrinth from the perspective of a consumer. At the same time, the marketing department for each product in question knows the intimate, exact details of their core product.

PRODUCT DEVELOPMENT
Let's move over to the product development perspective and look at how innovation on a product level unfolds. For now, we can leave business models and marketing schemes behind and simply look at the product.

I often like to refer to the core production line of the company. The important question is: what is the value produced and for whom? In the example of the moisturizer, the value would be in claiming a given market share, new or pre-existing. That could be the main goal of the entire corporate organization globally. No matter what the product is, the goal is to gain, keep, and ultimately increase a defined market share.

PRODUCTION OPTIMIZATION

From a product development perspective, it may be as important to focus on the production process as the market share. Let's take a deep dive into an average production facility around the world. An encompassing factor from this perspective would be the cost of producing the product versus the quality achieved in the product. Often, the efficiency of the production line is crucial. It is a goal *to produce the maximum number of products with the best possible quality in the shortest amount of time.*

Efficiency may also be measured by reduced waste from the production environment, the number of working hours involved in the production of each product unit, or the amount of energy used to produce each final product entity. Each business may have its own unique perspective on what production efficiency means to them. As long as the company can measure significant production efficiency through measurable key performance indicators (KPIs), that is what it takes to optimize the core production line.

It does not matter if it is a global cosmetic firm, a Hollywood film production company, a hairdresser, or a furniture manufacturing site. *The efficiency parameters of cost versus quality and time remain universal,* regardless of the product in question. Keep in mind that this principle also applies to any service. This is because a service also manifests similarly to a product in terms of cost, quality, and time required to be performed. Any other form of efficiency parameter beyond cost, quality, and time may be measured at will. The main point is that a KPI needs to be clearly defined and measurable. In total, the high-level universal approach towards core production optimization is the same whether the output is measurable in the form of a product or a service.

It is vital to vigilantly monitor production efficiency to understand where value creation exists. The value is not always immediately visible at first glance to outsiders. An example: I bought a new sofa for my living room, and I like to keep my eyes on the product I paid for. Is it comfortable to sit on? Does it hold the quality I expect for a given price? Is the supply chain of the factory production line sustainable, and does the product use renewable raw materials? The sustainability quality seal has recently become an important new part of the original product—in this case, a sofa. What may have seemed like a static product like a sofa to me now consists of more interchangeable values and qualities. It is crucial for the business to understand the different aspects the consumer values in the core product being brought to market. These aspects are where innovation should happen.

Many executives may think their core production value chain and core business model are completely obvious and need not be discussed further. Still, a surprising number of executives do not understand the shift in relevant core production value chains or core business models dictating their existing market. Also, it is probably necessary for a greater part, if not all, of the business organization to understand where their business is situated in the greater market space. A CEO may probe the awareness and understanding of the various role owners in the different layers of the organization. What do they think is the core production value chain and core business model?

ORGANIZATIONAL PERSPECTIVES ON A PRODUCT

If one asks different leadership roles in any large organization what the core product of the business is, one may be surprised to hear how different the responses can be. The replies often tend to reflect the core responsibility area of each person. Using a global cosmetic firm's product launch as an example, the different vantage points on core value creation may vary as follows:

- Chief Technical Officer (CTO): "Our aim is to technically create the best moisturizing cream in the market we serve."

- Chief Marketing Officer (CMO): "Our aim is to have a 40% market share with our products."

- Chief Operating Officer (COO): "Our aim is to have the best organization and product facilities to produce the top moisturizing cream."

In short, it is a human trait to project one's own perspective on a matter to one's immediate surroundings and often globally. We may all articulate our subjective perspectives as truths, even when we don't intend to.

It is a human balancing act to judge how far from our own person our perspectives are valid in every area of life.

It is important for the CEO to understand exactly what the core product is, what the core production line should be, and what the design of the organization should look like. The CEO leads the organization to deliver the best product of the best quality at a given cost to the largest market. This includes facilitating a shared view of what a potential product launch will provide on every level, both low and high. This is a balancing act that reaches far inside the organization as well as externally. It also includes navigating the organization according to the requirements of the owners. Many employees may form opinions about their leadership based on what they see going on between the CEO and the organization, while the CEO's focus must be on the owners' terms and related communication as much as on the internal workings.

Much of the organization will focus on their own parts of the production line, core or not. At the same time, internal roles often do not fully take into account what is supportive and what is at the core of the business. The CEO needs to have both a grounded and an encompassing perspective on this, as well as understanding the vantage points of other roles in the organization. If any part of the organization is not clearly observing what the aim of their role is and how that aim relates to the overall strategy of the company, then communication and the development of a shared understanding need to take place.

This distinction between what is a capability and what is a product offering is often missed by large parts of the organization. It takes a competent CEO to communicate internally and externally what the core product of the organization is in a way that is fruitful for all. Sometimes this is surprisingly unclear, and at other times it is less important that absolutely everyone in the company is aware of it. For every person and department involved in innovation, it is useful to understand where in the production process and value chain they are situated and contributing so that the direction of innovation can be cohesive, shared, aligned, and purposeful.

Did you ever try to work with a colleague who kept focusing on something that seemed unimportant to you? One example is HR processes, which may constitute the foundation of the company. Most companies cannot survive without some form of HR services available. Most would probably not want to work for a company without high-quality HR processes. Still, most staff functions are somewhat distant from the core business. HR and other examples of staff functions like finances, support services, and internal IT may seem less important to some product managers, but cumulatively, they are important supportive acts for the core production line. When we think of it, supporting services such as cleaning, security, and reception work are all building services, but if these are not performed to satisfaction, it may not only hamper the core production line but may also bring business to a grinding halt. During the pandemic of 2020–2022, many of us got used to working from home, but without a well-functioning IT service supporting us, the picture of business survival would have been very different.

INNOVATION LEADING TO COMPLEX BUSINESS MODELS

Let's look at some of the fastest-growing companies during the last ten years and their business models: Financial Technology (fintech), for example, and their payment solutions in particular. The competitive landscape has changed drastically as innovation has led to new business models and the buildup of new types of assets for many companies, often in the form of new datasets. It also makes sense to look at how the value chains[7] of product offerings have changed and expanded with the introduction of data as an asset in numerous areas of business. According to Wikipedia, a value chain refers to an overview of all activities within a company. In this context, I refer to a value chain as an identified process or chain of activities that provides tangible value.

One example is the Norwegian company Vipps, one of many payment solution apps that have surfaced internationally over the last few years. DnB, a Norwegian bank, invested in and developed the smartphone payment app Vipps as a local response to global payment apps and services. DnB invested in Vipps knowing they would not receive a cut of each transaction from the app's end-users. Vipps was, and still is, commercial-free, so there is also no direct income through ads from related commercial players.

The reason for DnB to create this new product can be seen from a few angles. First, Vipps was a local reaction to emerging global payment apps, with the intention of capturing a new market space. DnB could not possibly have known the entire future landscape of how payment apps would evolve when Vipps was launched in 2015, but they did know that they had to act in the app payment space as a way not to fall behind in a fast-developing fintech landscape. The idea of data as an asset in itself was

---

7   https://en.wikipedia.org/wiki/Value_chain

a trend that DnB understood well enough to take action on. DnB was not first to the market, but by coming roughly second, they gained a clear idea of what they wanted to achieve. DnB managed to capture the Norwegian home country for smartphone payment apps. In a matter of months, Vipps gained 1.4 million users in a country of five million people.

DnB expanded its potential client base substantially since many of the Vipps users were clients of competing banks. A new space in fintech opened up this opportunity for DnB, who managed to lengthen their value chain and hence their delivery model. Concurrently, they gained control as they acquired unique insights into the user patterns of 1.4 million users nationwide.

This is simply one example of how an innovative business model can expand the existing product and service value chain for a company. By daring to go early to market with an innovative product while not being the first, DnB hit the exact right time and business model to take a lion's share of the market in Norway for this kind of app.

The expansion of business models by adding various types of data to almost any business that can be digitized has increased exponentially across the planet during the last decade. This wave of introducing data as an asset is innovative in itself and has opened the opportunity to expand existing value chains in so many ways. Facebook was innovative in its time by introducing an online socializing platform that earned money with page ads. Innovations, including data, have moved fast since Facebook launched.

Looking back, it is peculiar to see how Facebook managed to gain access to so much information about almost three billion people, including data points on relationships, personal movement, photos, and consumer habits, when intelligence bureaus have probably tried to do the same for decades without getting even close. By offering a digital version of each person's unique network and relationships and the tools to maintain them online, people were willing to share these with a private digital actor.

Today, only human fantasy limits the utilization of new datasets emerging as human existence is increasingly digitized. The parallel commercialization of artificial intelligence (AI), the Internet of Things (IoT), big data, and machine learning (ML) has brought unprecedented opportunity for new business models based on new constellations of datasets. Cheap hardware enables the scaling of data collection. Data collection combined with a mature understanding of how the capitalization of old and new datasets is turned into ever-new assets is changing the way we live our lives. Various business value chains and product offerings for consumer goods have expanded. The human mind and understanding of how the world should work have been shaken, particularly by and for the young. The way we learn, interact, behave, and even think today is to a large extent the result of a data-driven, commercial development that is still accelerating.

CAPABILITY VS PRODUCT OFFERING

In many organizations, innovation applied to internal processes and production lines or to the external product offering and market can result in coincidental altered KPIs in both. For example, a COO of a water management facility may focus on quality improvement of water pipes with operational equipment maintenance in mind. The effects of such quality measures may also result in costs saved per cubic meter of water processed. In addition, each cubic meter of processed water will have improved quality as it exits the water tap of the end consumer. By using new materials and fresh coatings in the water piping infrastructure, both reductions in product costs and increased product quality are achieved. By improving the production environment parameter, external desirable outputs are realized. Often, changes applied to one part of the product, service, or organization will affect other parts independently, whether such consequences are known or not up front.

Another example is a Chief Information Officer (CIO) who introduces the use of GitHub for internal software development, which results in faster and higher-quality programming. Such an improvement may be measured in both increased efficiency for each in-house software programmer as well as improved quality and robustness in the code of the finished software product. At times, management sees the benefit of innovation and the related internal investments through the lenses of his or her role, while the actual effects go beyond the initial intention. The way the KPI is aimed at and measured may not completely reflect how internal risks and production efficiencies are influenced, as well as the product quality. The way effects are measured in the internal production line may not take improved product quality into consideration. It becomes an additional benefit.

This also works the other way around. By keeping the end product in mind and focusing on lowering production costs or making improvements to the internal production line, the operational environment may be improved.

For example, in the area of health, safety, security, and quality (HSSQ), it is not that all ripple effects are unknown or uncharted by management upfront. Focusing on specific KPIs and returns on investments drives the desired change in the first place.

I believe it can be beneficial to recognize and understand more about the various areas of value creation of a product or service than what many managers and executives perceive before exploring reinvestments. It may suffice for leadership to know that the production process and product are enhanced. The financial result is positive in either case. It can be useful to actively maneuver feedback loops of data separately when it comes to working with improved production processes, improved organizational processes, and an improvement of the product itself. By adding granularity and perspective to how the business looks inward at itself and its product in a changing market, there is a growing opportunity to innovate. Taking a look at the big picture reveals what matters most and where the effects will be most profound and lasting. I will get back to this later in this book. In "Part 3," I will explain how the mapping of values can be instrumental in pinpointing where innovation should be directed internally in the business, product, or organization.

WHERE TO START

First, what is a use case? I have already referred to use cases several times, and upon some reflection, I prefer the simplicity of how Wikipedia describes it to be one of the two[8]:

1. A usage scenario for a piece of software; often used in the plural to suggest situations where a piece of software may be useful.

2. A potential scenario in which a system receives an external request (such as user input) and responds to it.

In short, and in my own words, a use case is a case where you use something in a systematic way to achieve a specific result. It is a rather general term; it refers to a system in a way that is flexible, scalable, and does not limit the system's thinking to any small or large setting. Every time I use a system to perform any kind of activity where I expect a certain output, in my theory, that is a use case. When I am in the supermarket, the cashier resolves the use case of technically paying for my groceries. I expect a use case to perform some kind of action for someone. A system that returns any kind

---

8   https://en.wikipedia.org/wiki/Use_case

of tangible value through its actions. The term use case is usually coined to refer to the development of software systems that resolve or perform certain systematic actions that return some kind of value, but I like to think of it in a wider sense. To me, a use case can include analog systems that create tangible value.

The distinction, or likeness, between analog innovation and digital innovation should be clear for anyone working with use cases. Speaking about innovation, many assume we are talking about digital innovation. Or at least innovation by developing digitized use cases. I consider the split between traditional innovation and digital innovation to be mostly an illusion, constructed by digitalized organizations and communities around the world. **I believe the largest difference between analog innovation and digital innovation is the tools and assets available to the creative process.**

The creative value chain of digital innovations may also be new to most of us. Digitization opens up new landscapes globally where emerging markets and new business models evolve with increasing speed. New technologies have always disrupted our lives, from the application of fire to the development of the wheel, the electric grid, and the introduction of interconnectivity in the form of the internet. The disruption a new value chain opens up is unknown and enquiring. It takes time for civilizations to regulate and get used to disruptive technologies. Until the application and commercial use of new technologies are commonplace for the majority of members of society, most will not completely comprehend the effects of the new technology.

Nor how the resulting innovation and use cases will affect business models and markets. The concept of digital transformation has been around as a buzzword for several years, referring to the global shift towards digitalization. Most are still grappling to come to terms with the new landscape where new solutions to old problems evolve and what innovative value chains look like. **I hear many who refer to disruptive tech, and often I suspect the topic discussed really is disruptive business models and not the new application of technology in itself.**

According to TrueQC, digitization describes the pure analog-to-digital conversion of existing data and documents. Digitization does not seek to optimize the processes or applications of data. Gartner defines digitalization as "the use of digital technologies to change

Diagram 1

AI Use Cases

Describing the shift from analog to digital use case development processes.

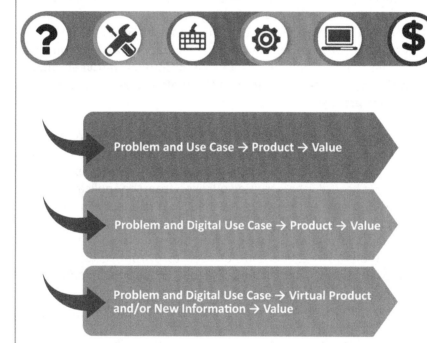

Problem and Use Case → Product → Value

Problem and Digital Use Case → Product → Value

Problem and Digital Use Case → Virtual Product and/or New Information → Value

The largest difference between analog innovation and digital innovation is the tools and assets available to the creative process. Any part of a use case can be digitized, and it is up to the innovator and the circumstances to decide how each use case and solution should be composed. There are no absolute rules to this process, and the gradual change from analog to digital may be a natural way to proceed.

a business model and provide new revenue and value-producing opportunities; it is the process of moving to a digital business."

Consider the paper clip. This is a highly analog invention. The structural process of this innovation is as follows:

→ *Problem and use case* → *Product* → *Value*

In this case, data, information, or insight is not the actual product. The paperclip is analog and physical, made up of a twisted piece of metal string. This is how human innovation has been working for thousands of years, from the invention of the wheel to the useful paperclip of our times. Someone simply sees a need and builds a solution to resolve a defined problem.

If we look at a pharmaceutical firm optimizing a cosmetic product, we are still working with a physical end product, while the use case may be digital. This would be the case when pieces of information in the form of datasets are applied to machine learning models. Potentially, the use case could be to optimize the application of an expensive cosmetic ingredient to provide the desired effect of the final product while staying within budgetary limits. The use case may be digital when there is a physical product involved. The use case input is digital, while the actual product enhancement is physical. In this case, the structure of innovation will look like the following:

→ *Problem and digital use case* → *Product* → *Value*

The use cases that have been entirely digital in recent years are often the ones that gain the most attention. Social networks online are examples of such use cases. They are revolutionary and disruptive compared to the earlier thousands of years of innovation because the product itself is digitized. Facebook revolutionized our world by shifting many of our friendships from the analog world to the digital sphere. Our digital relationships are still a real product, but we start getting entangled in business models where the value for the end-user and the service provider may differ greatly. While end-users consume digital friendships online, the service provider Facebook earns value not only through selling ads but also by reselling personal information for marketing purposes. This is when technology disrupts and widens the divide between what the end-user consumes and what the service or content provider sells. The use case structure, in this case, may be described as follows:

→ *Problem and digital use case* → *Virtual product and/or new information*
→ *Value*

The virtual products here are insight and influence. Globally, there is a growing divide between those with insight and those without it. The information age is evolving fast and creating new divides between those who have it and those who do not. This new divide could turn out to be a determining factor, just as the divide between the educated and the illiterate was a hundred years ago. Being digital versus not being digital is a question of 'to be or not to be' for many people, organizations, and communities.

Select organizations and some resistant individuals are increasingly challenged to fulfill their life cycles to perfection without ever going digital. Analog lifestyles are disappearing as digitalization quickly expands to distant corners of the world. Digitizing a business, organization, or product is often a market benefit in itself. My prime example is my most recent electric toothbrush, which comes with an app that tells me what areas on my teeth or gums I may have missed. It seems no business or domain is immune from digital use cases. At least I have not come across any... yet.

Every consulting firm with a certain amount of respect for itself will offer various, yet perhaps not so varied, frameworks for digital transformation. All one needs to do is run a search for 'Use Case Development Plan,' and a dizzying amount of process charts, method descriptions, and slick slide decks appear. If one adds AI, big data, IoT, and ML to the mix, the search experience becomes even more daunting. During my two decades as a consultant, I have applied various methods. Ranging from IT project management frameworks to service management tools and a number of ISO standards to find the best practice and most fruitful way to obtain the required result. Best practices and project handbooks have been manifested as pillars for procuring the business results required. I have used best practices and frameworks as if there were a list I could pluck from for my own liking.

After all, every internal change project or product development plan should, in the end, benefit the financial top line or bottom line of the company. How to get there is often a subjective matter of preference. An improved product or enhanced service offering is the ultimate demand from executives, so methods and practices have always been a means to an end. Most methods and practices are domain-specific, while AI has introduced challenges on a higher level.

When AI scaled from industrial niche tools to commercial products and surfaced in the world of commercialized mainstream IT, the large consulting businesses followed suit. One can easily look up a lot of methodologies and processes online that constitute more or less a best practice around how the introduction of this 'new technology' should be handled. Still, more often than not, when I drill down far enough into different practices and frameworks, they are not detailed or structured enough to make innovation work successfully. Direction and the final aim are often not clear enough for all involved. There is room for interpretation as each organization and manufacturing floor works differently.

On the other hand, if a lot of detail is added to the innovative process, the momentum is often reduced, and the positive emotion oozing from fresh invention starts to evaporate as if too much structure dampens the human experience. The magic ingredient of creativity is often missing in the world of practices, frameworks, and methods. How can we best discover if the invigorating, innovative tool will actually be worth the investment and take the organization or business in the right direction?

No framework or method can bridge human uncertainty in uncharted territory, as innovation is ultimately perceived as something unknown for many business owners. Strong and charismatic leaders often make equally strong decisions and point out clear directions for all to follow. Think of how Elon Musk or Steve Jobs staked out a direction for so many based on visions they held and wanted to see realized. The balancing act between being a strong leader and becoming authoritarian can be challenging and requires continuous self-scrutiny. Strong leaders who turn authoritarian (or come across as authoritarian) run the risk of obstructing individual creativity and engagement in the organization. When individual creativity is stifled, the workforce turns dutiful to reach the goals of the company. The total effort of the organization becomes linear and increasingly loses flexibility and individual initiatives, for good and for bad. Many organizations aspiring to innovate aim for the subjectively required balance between efficiency and space for creativity.

As the world shifts towards new organizational ideals, individual strong leadership is not exactly becoming outdated, yet authoritarian leadership with a dictating communication style may lead to a stagnant organization in the long run. Today, co-creation and interconnectivity play a larger role in successful corporations than ever before. De-centralization of power and initiative is becoming the norm in an increasing number of business areas. Optimizing the potential realized both on an individual and collective level is steadily becoming more important. This redistribution of leadership opens up space for more potential to be realized in the overall organization, related communities, and markets.

As more innovative companies consider themselves parts of larger ecosystems, the rigidity of any structure not absolutely required can weigh down and slow processes and general creativity. The pace of change in business has picked up and is accelerating, while most corporations need to accelerate the changing pace in their organizations accordingly. Authoritarian leadership styles are, in general, increasingly unsuitable when it comes to disrupting markets. One person, even when at the top of the organization, can rarely keep up the pace required by all individuals collaborating and co-creating to reach fast-changing goals. Yet the conundrum remains: finding a balanced path between clear leadership and the enablement of individuals in the organization.

For many organizations and businesses following long-established rules of hierarchy, static frameworks are not sufficing anymore as competition is turning increasingly dynamic and agile. There are millions of consultants out there more than ready to hold the hand of their client, to help in applying the best possible method to the process, and to lead the way through new and changing times. The bad news is that not all of them have enough insight into what it takes to succeed with digital transformation in the disruptive markets of our current world. It is essential to be cautious and discern which one possesses enough insight in the areas needed to succeed with digital transformation in the disruptive markets of our current world as pertaining to your industry.

From an objective vantage point, general digitalization lacks an inside-out, balanced top-down and bottom-up approach. The innovator must be in balance with the context of the business without focusing too much on one aspect of a product. A more holistic approach based on principles has long been overdue. Any predefined method and framework may be a useful supportive tool to enable change, yet it eluded me until recently how to deal with the path of change that leads into the unknown.

The vision and goal of creating the world's best product will require strong leadership and clear communication internally and externally, while the change of culture required in organizations will require a softer hand and different means. The well-cited quote "Culture eats strategy for breakfast" by Peter Drucker aims to describe how company culture is essential for the success in realizing strategies. Building culture is often a slow process that, among many factors, requires leaders to set consistent examples over time. Relations and collaboration matter. Building the best product requires first a vision, then a culture and organization that are aligned in a shared direction, often facilitated by a strong leader and skilled communicator.

The less powerful the vision, the less need there is for a strong leader. After all, some organizations exist for the purpose of maintaining the status quo rather than changing the world. Your local waterworks may be better served by clear goals and KPIs than by world-changing visions. Continuous improvements may serve better in many cases for waterworks than ground-breaking disruption, even if I am convinced that happens at times too.

Cultural tolerance for change is something I often explore with consulting clients without necessarily telling them that I am gauging this factor as closely as I do. In my early days as a consultant, I often experienced pushback from the organization when implementing changes in processes, technology, or the organizational landscape. My eagerness to help the company improve business by introducing technology was often not welcomed in the way I had expected. Part of becoming a successful consultant was to learn to observe and understand how much real change the organization and stakeholders really wanted or could tolerate. Imagine the frustration when I improved the work processes of a work floor to be more efficient, and the consequences for the business side were negative. By introducing new tools and eliminating substantial parts of the production process, I reduced the required headcount on the production floor, and *voila*, my employers found themselves in conflict with the labor organizations. In some countries and organizations, this is an issue, while in other places it is less of an issue.

It is important to gauge the context of digital innovation when implementing changes, as the consequences may be unforeseen if the change is truly successful. In this context, culture is a huge factor in what is considered successful digital innovation and what is not.

STRATEGY, TACTICS, AND OPERATIONS ARE PILLARS

While strategy, tactics, and execution emerged as concepts more than a hundred years ago in the military science of warfare, the Roman Emperor Julius Caesar[9] was already a famous military strategist 2000 years ago. Today, the terms are generally accepted in business and form important parameters for leadership in a changing world. Strategy, tactics, and execution (execution is often referred to in organizations as operations) make up a framework in its own right when it comes to understanding the different levels of navigating a business. The depth level such a structure provides is something I look at as a prerequisite when actively innovating. I always try to actively know where I am on that depth meter. Any efficient leader needs to know how to navigate and operate at the three levels of strategy, tactics and operations. It is not only for generals to find a balancing act between the three.

It is hugely helpful to keep the overall *what, how, and why* separate for anyone working with change. When dealing with new technology, it is as important as ever to understand if one works on the strategic, tactical, or operative plane. If this is not clear, one can easily get stuck with lofty ideas and over-simplified sketches that will never bear fruit. Without a strategy in place, one can stay immersed in the daily 'how-to' questions without ever developing a proper view of the direction, aim, and meaning of the business.

It makes sense that innovation happens at every level of thinking, from the highest level of a 100-year perspective business plan (yes, they do exist) down to the most mundane level of resolving a basic 'how-to' problem. The practice of putting a man on the moon is, of course, very far from inventing and making the first paper clip. Still, for innovation to create real impact, I believe it is important to be conscious of where in this depth meter the innovation should take place and actually takes place. Time and complexity of both use case and context matter. Sure, many small inventions, like the paper clip, have made a difference and have been used by billions of people. When inventing a product, it makes sense to understand the business driver of the invention and maintain awareness of the strategic, tactical, and operational plans.

So where does it make sense to start? When abstract ideas and operational questions are buzzing between different boxes and levels in a best practice framework, that does not resolve a new venture. I propose to start with

---

9   https://en.wikipedia.org/wiki/Julius_Caesar

three universal questions before even looking at the use case or product, the organization, or the process:

1. What do you want to achieve?

2. What product or result seriously matters, and why?

3. Do you have the information needed to achieve what you want? And do you have it in the form of data?

These are basic starting questions when innovating in the space of creating new digital use cases. There is a more granular path of exploration to come in this book, in "Part 3," but this is the best place to start. As innovators often come up with improvement ideas and suggestions for activities, it makes sense to ask these three questions about any new or existing measures being evaluated.

With the three simple questions above, we are working in the strategic sphere as well as checking our bases. If you have worked with your definitions of vision and mission in a framework, that is a good place to start asking these questions. Several frameworks profess these first questions in unison.

Balanced Scorecard (BSC)[10] is a strategic planning and performance management framework that aims to measure where you are and where you are going in a directional way. Balanced Scorecard provides useful principle-based stepping stones on a strategic level. They are not the same as the stepping stones I apply in this book, beyond the first question: *What do you want to achieve?* Balanced Scorecard is a great tool, but alone it is too high-level to work efficiently with product innovation. By applying strategic tools alone, the path towards realizing value will become nebulous for most organizations.

I am not sure if it is always necessary to have strong control over direction and depth of thought before innovation can take place. I believe it can be hugely useful to actively navigate the strategic realm by applying strategic tools, while certain 'looseness' is required to innovate in a business-driven landscape. Agile[11] is all in vogue these days, and yet an overarching goal or strategy for the business needs to form the foundation for any real

---

10   https://en.wikipedia.org/wiki/Balanced_scorecard
11   https://en.wikipedia.org/wiki/Agile

direction to be taken. Agile often refers to how project management and software development are executed, while the basic principles of agile involve shorter, cyclic work patterns replacing long-term static plans. Static, waterfall-structured methods are increasingly replaced by the active use of KPIs and dynamic deliverables.

By solving one problem at a time, the path to the goal is created. The organization works in increasingly interconnected ways towards a shared goal while suitably sized teams resolve a measured number of tasks at a time. Strategic business goals are highly useful to make good products thrive, while the best product in the world may still fail without the direction of strategic business goals to stake out a place in the market.

Many methods and frameworks used by global consulting firms take an agile approach towards innovation. Their methods often start by defining a tangible problem to be solved. From there, the process moves on to frame the value to be created and the feasibility of resolving the problem. Then a defined, innovative container for further work is created.

This is a good start, but I believe further systematic granularity needs to be applied. Both to anticipate (and articulate) the real value of innovation as well as to create meaningful KPIs for value creation as early as possible in the innovation process. The feasibility of a use case is clearly an essential factor, even if it is not directly translatable to asking the question of whether the necessary data or information is available or not. It is surprising how often the use case quickly becomes more tangible when asking for data and information than when asking about almost anything else. Asking for data and information is most relevant when working with IT, in particular with models involving AI, IoT, big data, and ML. Availability and access to data or information are crucial for any digital change or digital product development leading to innovation. If IT systems containing data are not sufficiently accessible and aligned with the organization and core production line, the business will struggle to innovate efficiently in the area of IT.

KNOW WHERE YOU ARE IN YOUR OWN LANDSCAPE
In parallel to understanding the organization's alignment of strategy, tactics, and operation, it is equally important to understand the organization's capabilities versus product offerings. By capabilities, I mean any resource or service that serves the organization internally. By product offering, I point to anything the organization will offer to the outside world that brings revenue or some form of value to your organization.

A business plan[12] can be a useful tool for mapping both capabilities and product offerings. A business plan, no matter how simple, may also reveal whether the intended value will support the strategy of the organization or business.

Over the last decade, I have found the LEAN Business Canvas[13] tool immensely useful to navigate and plan for any new stream of business or grasp new ideas for value creation in the form of internal capability or a product or service offering. Business plans, as lengthy documents, are increasingly getting outdated as their form becomes superfluous. If you would like to explore the business methodology of LEAN[14], particularly in the space of how to make an organization create something new under conditions of uncertainty, I would recommend the book, *The Lean Startup: How Today's Entrepreneurs Use Continuous Innovation to Create Radically Successful Businesses* by Eric Ries.

The focus of this chapter is to explore the context of intentional innovation and how to create a sound path to increase the return on your investment. By observing where you are in the landscapes of organization and market space, it will be easier to work efficiently. The internal and external vantage points for innovation should not be static. While some strategies stay in place for decades, centuries, and even millennia, others change far more frequently. It can be useful to work with continuous improvement across the board to ensure alignment is taking place top-down or bottom-up, navigating every direction of the landscape.

By introducing agile methodology, which results in newer, much faster iterations of product development, the focus on AS-IS (current state) analysis has weakened increasingly over the last few years. When driving innovation, it often matters less to look past former benchmarks. Relevant KPIs are often nonexistent. When aiming for disruptive business models and disruptive tech, be aware and cautious about using outdated KPIs for the organization and business.

It makes sense to spend as little work as possible on mapping out descriptions of where a company and its employees are before moving towards the future. Knowing where you are when you start, without having to write an entire history book on the past, you can simply move

---

12   https://en.wikipedia.org/wiki/Business_plan
13   https://en.wikipedia.org/wiki/Business_Model_Canvas
14   https://en.wikipedia.org/wiki/Lean

forward. Still, a certain amount of understanding of the current situation Is necessary to have a solid foundation to work from. This is a balancing act in itself, and every organization, business, and company will need to find the right balance between agility and robustness when it comes to a change of pace and innovation. As market demands change, the pace and turn of strategic direction change faster than ever. Leadership and organizations both need to adapt. Too dynamic of an approach and the required robustness may suffer, while too much robustness may slow the pace of the enterprise down in a fast-moving market.

It is necessary to know in which part of the organization innovation will be most efficient and return the most value. We are talking about the overarching three areas of enterprise: product or service, or the production environment.

Many companies decide to innovate, particularly in the form of introducing new technology, in processes without being discerning enough regarding the aim and result of the investment. It may seem tempting, with lower risk attached, to introduce new technology far away from the core business, core production, or core process. To me, the example of starting innovation in the area of HR or service management is a classic way to not realize the large potential of return on investment (ROI). For many organizations, digitizing internal HR processes or introducing robotic process automation[15] (RPA) functions in the service management process seem like steps in the right direction.

In this way, they avoid risk on behalf of anything close to the core product or core production line. Unfortunately, the return of such non-critical innovation is usually of far less value to the company than what it could have been if the innovation was pointed at the core production line or product. It may look like risk is a necessary evil when innovating and introducing change, yet I would claim that to be not true at all. Innovation handled in a controlled manner works best when it is cleverly targeted where the impact is the greatest.

The exact sweet spot of impactful innovation can be disparate across different organizations and businesses. The first step towards achieving value is to build up a reasoned point of view on where it makes sense to innovate in the company. Innovation may be focused on the organization itself by building internal capabilities related to the core production

---

15   https://en.wikipedia.org/wiki/Robotic_process_automation

line or by innovating directly on the product itself. For most production companies, the effect of innovation is maximized when it focuses directly on the product going to market. That said, many service companies that change work processes through innovation provide more value than improved processes themselves.

One example of such a service process change would be an automated check-in process in hotels. An automated check-in process disrupts the work process of the reception clerk by removing the entire process. At the same time, it may reduce the check-in time for the guest, who is the most important service end-user in this context. For companies extracting natural resources, for instance, mining companies, the best way to maximize returns on innovation may be to work on the core production line and specific production bottlenecks in the extraction of a product.

These are merely two examples of where it makes sense to innovate. So far, there is no known given logic or proven set of rules that can determine which of the three areas—organization, production line, or product—innovation will provide the most value. For some time, I experimented with the hypothesis that there would be a difference between various industries yielding high returns on innovation. I suspected oil and gas production companies would have an increased innovation rate compared to other businesses with lower margins, for instance in the areas of transport and logistics, where margins are lower.

Ultimately, it is unclear how certain industries would be more likely to create value through innovation than others. My idea of financial opportunity for innovation as a driver folded, as many companies with a steady income and secure market shares would be more complacent than their competitors about making changes. In parallel, companies working with stretched business models and far smaller margins would need to innovate with minimal resources just to survive in tough competitive landscapes. The theory of change is a psychological factor in most industries, and it is tricky to make any predictions about the scale and speed of successful innovation upfront.

It is perfectly possible to observe gaps between innovation rates in various industries. It can be an interesting exercise to try to point out business areas where one would have expected innovation to happen earlier than it actually does. But there are often complex or strong reasons driving the status quo in such cases, and for most of us, it is tricky to simply guess where and when future innovation may be most beneficial. Innovation has similar qualities to an uncharted land. Even if one can shape and introduce new ideas in various ways, the exact scale and speed of achieving what is wanted in the end may vary from any plan business leaders choose. That is why it is called innovation; the change is new to the world and has not been realized before.

So, when setting out to explore the new and unknown, it is necessary to have an opinion, a point of view, or even a hypothesis of what will work and why. Without it, one will not easily know the depth of thought one is working at. There is a risk of missing the possibility of an optimized new product or service that is a fit for the organization, the market, the team doing the innovation, or the potential end-users.

The human dream of flying has been a vision shared by a number of individuals, ranging from Leonardo da Vinci to the Wright brothers, who realized the first human fixed-wing flight on December 17th, 1903. Their first flight in Kitty Hawk, North Carolina, lasted 12 seconds and reached a range of 36 meters. It may seem like a small feat today, yet it is a stellar example of how a *vision* matures into a tangible *goal* and finally into reality.

Their hypothesis of human flight was crystal clear. Wilbur and Orwille Wright formulated their own *strategy* for human flight with their fixed-wing aircraft and then moved on to *tactics* and *action*, resulting in what many consider a milestone for humanity: the start of the era of human flight. Their path of *vision, goal, strategy, tactics, and action* comprises a stellar example of hypothesis-driven innovation. Without vision, there will be no goals, and without goals, there will be no good ways to measure progress and achievement. Action needs to be underpinned and have frontrunners before it can support any vision.

With this backdrop on digital transformation, "Part 3" of the book will move on to more tangible steps towards how to succeed with digital transformation. Keeping a close eye on the parameters that matter throughout transformation is crucial, and to assist, frameworks and best practices may be of support on the digital journey. Context is helpful to understand the environment and conditions for change. The navigation tools that follow are necessary to create security in changing environments.

We leave circumstances behind and move on to tangible tools for maneuvering digital change in "Part 3" of this book. "Part 3" will build on the conditions laid out in "Part 1" and "Part 2" and move on to introduce more substantial advice. So far, the discovery of transformation has been at the center, while in the next part, it is time to venture on to the *how* of digital transformation and use case development.

PART 3

NAVIGATING THE EVOLUTION
OF USE CASES

THE NINE STEPS OF USE CASE EVALUATION

When developing use cases, it has generally been common to look at the *available data* along with the practical *viability* of the development and the potential *value* of the use case. This overarching approach to navigating three complimentary parameters is a 100% improvement compared to using no structured method. I would like to add a lot more detail and specificity to the way digital innovation works beyond these three steps. It is a continuous challenge to work efficiently and at the right level with the right granularity that makes sense without digging into too much detail in the process. The upside of working exclusively with the triangular questions of data, viability, and value would be to impose as few limitations as possible when working with use case development. In this way, a minimum of constraints are imposed in the early phase of use case development, leading to innovation.

The downside of such a wide approach is that the first few initial use case ideas that surface, which may seem like good ideas to start with, can soon become the entire strategy and plan. A minimum of nuanced scrutiny should be applied to validate each use case according to specific constraints and opportunities. Subjectivity in use case development is not necessarily a bad thing, yet I want to offer a complimentary and deepening set of use case qualifications for identifying and validating any digital use case. The method needs to be universal while also

covering as much of the specific landscape of use case development as possible. It is crucial to hit the sweet spot between high and low-level thinking. The creation of value in itself is not concerned with whether the original thought was conceived at a strategic, tactical, or operational level.

The following nine steps set out to do exactly that—capture as much detail as possible as early as possible without wasting time or resources on the path to innovation.

1. PROBLEM

Most data scientists would argue that the first place to look for a use case is in the data. Similarly, most business developers or CFOs would argue that the very first place to look would be to identify an important and real problem to be solved by data. For the CFO, there would be a need for the problem in question to be business-related in some form. If the problem to be solved will not impact business, then the value of the use case will not be worth pursuing. For a domain expert, such as an operational controller on the production floor, the use case will become relevant when it resolves or improves a practical problem.

In my experience, any problem driving a use case will need to be a real human problem. If it is not, then it will be challenging to convey the value it will produce for the end-user, and the consequent buy-in from the business side will be absent. To put it in other words, if the use case does not solve a human problem, it will be close to impossible to communicate the value to another human. Where technology stands today, the human understanding of the problem is as validating for the use case as the nature of the problem itself. A sound human understanding of the potential value will need to be established for the use case to be developed.

Let's go through an example of a use case involving data mining. A building management firm would like to save energy, and the root cause for proposing this use case would be to reduce the cost of heating the building mass. The idea is that by installing sensors and collecting status on doors, one will be able to detect open doors, allowing the heat inside to escape. Such insight could also enable further value from self-closing mechanisms already installed on doors for safety reasons, given that this mechanism could be monitored and operated remotely from a central location. It is my belief that it is useful to identify the problem of open doors before looking for the data needed for a use case.

Still, if another person would look at the existing data, for instance, tracking power bills and the growing cost of power consumption, one could perfectly well deduce a path into the same use case by starting to look at the available data first. Then it would become clear what data would be available right away to support the use case (power bills) and what other datasets could be wished for to add value to the use case (door sensors reporting door status). Sensors that used to be costly are now widely available and are often becoming cheaper by the year, making the introduction of new datasets a viable option when developing use cases.

The problem needs to be verified upfront during the use case development and definitely before the use case is scaled. It makes sense to ask the business side, in the form of a product owner or operations executive, for validation before work is initiated to develop the use case. If management does not find the problem important enough to invest in, then the use case may be parked.

We have all heard of smart people who innovated something immensely important by chance or by understanding the importance of technical invention itself and what it would bring to the world. The truth is that when technical inventions are made for the technology itself, a strike of luck is needed for them to provide a valid use case for the business side and become successful.

Even Thomas Edison would most likely not have fully understood the exact potential of the light bulb he invented at the time of his life-changing idea. He understood its potential and knew the direction in which his invention would contribute to humanity, but the scale of success could not be known upfront. It would resolve a tangible, communicable problem that was clear to all, and exactly that shared understanding of the human problem was what made the light bulb so successful. The window of opportunity for the light bulb was provided by the availability of the materials needed to create the product and the mass consumption of electricity, which was new at the time. The possibility for people, in particular the workforce, to extend what used to be daytime activities and productivity into the evening and night was the real driver for the success of the light bulb. In the same way, the need to reduce power bills is the underlying driver for the use case of door automation in a building management firm.

A human and tangible problem provides for clear communication of the value of the use case to immediate stakeholders and to the marketplace.

My claim is that every successful use case has the capacity, or potential, to resolve a real, tangible human problem. If the idea of a solution to a problem is not well communicated or shared appropriately with all relevant stakeholders, the use case is likely to fizzle, no matter how real the potential value of it is. The human factor of the problem to be resolved is a key success factor.

2. DATA

Is relevant data available to resolve the problem? This should be the first question asked for any data-driven use case. Before the days of digitized information technology (IT), the question might be changed to: *Are there relevant materials available to resolve the problem?* Understanding the parallel between materials in the past and digital pieces of information today may make it easier to understand how datasets impact innovation in our world. I have encountered many senior executives challenged to comprehend this parallel understanding of what seem to be two separate spheres of innovation, each adding layers of context through different époques in history.

Innovation of a material nature is still going strong. Material inventions have been disruptive and commercialized for as long as humans have existed. Concept development involving datasets has also existed for a long time, yet the volume, complexity, and commercialization have expanded exponentially for a few decades and have come to a point where it makes our world simply look different than before. The introduction of telecommunications took place more than a hundred years ago. More recently, the introduction of mobile smartphones has brought the original idea of speaking remotely to an entirely new level by providing access to remote data. This shift involving data has not only changed the world we operate in, but it has also changed us, humans, at least as much in the way we operate.

The access to continuous new types of data in the form of new datasets as well as the increased size of such datasets combined with the availability of new materials and products have all opened an unprecedented number of windows of enormous size and potential impact on our lives. In a pointed way, one can claim that the only thing that changed in innovation during the last 100 years was that data in itself has been isolated as an asset to the extent of driving one of the most massive emerging economies humanity has ever seen. This new window of opportunity opened by the explosive evolution of datasets is not rocket science in itself. It is only our imagination that sets limitations on what use cases may be developed in the years to come.

As world markets are dazzled by the novelty of the situation, it is easy to be lured to think that data is the driver for innovation when it really is the enabler. The human problems that new data can resolve are still the drivers of new use cases worldwide. This will not change until the world is no longer human-centered but has become machine-centered. Did you ever watch the movie *The Matrix*? As I write this book, almost 24 years have passed since it was released, and its success has in many ways evolved around portraying a world that has become machine-centered and left the human-centric model behind. No wonder it was so provocative when it was released, while today teenagers barely flinch at the apparent shift from human centricity to machine centricity in the way the movie portrays.

So, the existential question for every digital use case remains: *Is there relevant data available to resolve the problem?* For any use case, this question needs to be addressed with no hesitation, as there will be no successful use case without it. I would compare it to building a car without the right materials, or at best with materials of low-grade quality. If data is not available in a given space, no digitalization will take place there. It seems obvious, but the lack of sufficient or adequate data is often the major obstacle to successful digital innovation.

3. VALUE

When there is an articulated problem and relevant data available to work with, then it is time to work towards a clear hypothesis of value creation. Sometimes an observed problem and the following search for data are the result of a desire for value creation in the first place. For instance, a common question will be: *How can a company save money on the core production line while maintaining the desired production efficiency and quality of the product?* Here we already have three different types of value: saving money, production efficiency, and product quality. It can be useful to keep the focus on each of these three parameters separately. I like to work from two different vantage points on value creation when I work with use cases:

- Hypothesis-driven use case development
- Value stream[16] breakdown

---

16   https://en.wikipedia.org/wiki/Value-stream_mapping

According to Wikipedia, value stream maps show the flow of both materials and information as they progress through a process. In this sense, a value stream map also represents a core business process that adds value to a material product. Value streams should not be interchanged with value chains, which are referred to as a way to show an overview of all activities within a company. In the context of this book, I refer to value stream breakdown as a way of breaking down any stream (or process) that creates a specific value for the organization or business. Hypothesis-driven use case development is a structured approach where a minimum of the structured process is applied to recognize where in the landscape of value creation a use case is currently located. Both hypothesis-driven use case development and value stream breakdown are further described below.

→ Looking away from the process
Hypothesis-driven use case development and value stream breakdown are commonly used in production environments and are applied as analytical processes in relation to operational processes in some form. In this book, I intend to work as free from any process as possible. I believe businesses over the last decades have been overwhelmed by process improvements. The LEAN framework and LEAN thinking, as well as any other process-oriented change management, have long been the hype for several global business consultancies. Improvement work on internal processes has turned out to be useful for many, yet I sometimes sense that real, and harder, changes are avoided for the sake of continuous process improvement.

When an organization has continuously improved its internal processes for several decades, the question arises: *Are they done at any point?* Many organizations work with continuous process improvement as a concept, which for many may work well. Still, any larger or more painful change may keep being postponed as a result of the never-ending focus on process improvement. For top management, it can be easier to keep improving their internal processes as a way to avoid real and more pressing changes.

→ Moving beyond the already known
It is becoming increasingly clear to me that process in itself is often opposed to innovation. What questions can you ask to verify and ensure that you are moving beyond what you already know? *This is particularly poignant in the space of product and service development.* The strong focus on improving operational processes will often overshadow the way of thinking needed to make real changes in business models. Executives often make sure change is manageable within the existing organization. In this way, they

end up doing ever more internal projects for process improvement. This keeps them 'safe' and distanced from any form of disruptive change. When people claim to work with innovation, there will always be some form of process needed to contain and harvest the benefits of a use case. Applying more processes than absolutely necessary will often be counterproductive and push members of the organization away from the freedom of mind required to really think of something new and inventive.

The focus on AS-IS (current state) and TO-BE (future desired state) ensures that the path of change is as safe and predictable as possible, while such a focus inhibits the mind from working outside the pre-existing box. We humans can pull towards a known process in a conscious or unconscious attempt to gravitate towards something we know and already trust we can master. This gravitation towards safety will hamper new ways of thinking if we are not conscious of it. To think of the never-before-imagined is the most challenging thinking of all. Existing processes and contexts are challenging to move beyond. Sure, sometimes the most genius inventions consist of a minimum change to a long-known product, and *voila*, the new product is hugely innovative.

Once more, think of something as simple as a paper clip: a small string of metal bent into two oblong loops of different lengths. It would take 30 seconds to invent, in theory. The genius of the paperclip is that it resolves the very human problem of messy papers with immediate effect and ease. In addition, it is low-cost and widely available. It seems the biggest victory of the paper clip invention is its simplicity. Any complicated process around how it was invented would perhaps have diminished the value of the resulting product.

Also, the process of cleaning up any desk was not elaborated on but simplified by omitting big parts of the work process. The paper clip itself eliminates as much of the process of tidying loose papers as it possibly can. That's the purpose of it: not to make the process of cleaning a desk marginally easier, but to eliminate the process altogether where possible. It takes courage to be innovative. Any invention that removes a greater part of an operational process in place of altering it will psychologically tell any person who used to fulfill the original operational process that he or she may not be needed anymore. While the paper clip surely introduced some ease for paper clerks in its time, the introduction of digital information was, of course, seismic for office workers. The required skills to do routine paperwork changed dramatically as digital working skills were added.

However, the process of how the work was done would still remain largely similar to the former analog paper-pushing method.

Digital ledgers and spreadsheets replaced analog papers, while both old and new systems worked with the same columns, rows, and formulas for decades. ERP systems like SAP and Oracle have, in many ways, maintained legally required processes in the tools while slowly making the processes easier to work with through digital smarts. The manual processes of most accountants in the past have been digitized without too much change to the basic process. It may seem that the legal requirements of accounting require the process to remain the same, no matter if the task is performed analogically or digitally, but we do see how an increasing amount of automation, often in the form of RPA, keeps the required process to a minimum, at least for the person using the system.

Moving beyond the paper clip and RPA, another example of adding value through real innovation by cutting processes can be seen in the area of transportation, more recently often referred to as mobility. While maintenance and improvement of roads have been done for thousands of years and will continue as far into the future as we can imagine, the introduction of passenger air traffic shifted transport to an entirely new level because transportation options were shifted beyond the ground and sea and into the sky. The window of opportunity for airborne vehicles contributed to the business model of aircraft carriers transporting millions of people by air within a few decades following the invention of the aircraft carrier. Try to think of this innovation in the context of efficient human transportation and not in the context of how to improve the road network or how to make ships move more efficiently. In principle, that is the same as moving from operational process improvement to disruptive innovation. The rules of mobility have fundamentally changed. By leaving known concepts and processes behind, the space for free-thinking expands, and bigger shifts towards new business models can evolve.

Visions can emerge everywhere. Everyone can catch a bright idea while singing in the shower. I know of no borders outside of which visions and goals cannot operate. So, innovation also operates at all levels, and not one area can hold a monopoly on the greatness required for visions and innovations to grow and become real. In many ways, the United States Declaration of Independence includes the freedom to make visions and goals in the well-known phrase where it defends the individual right to

"Life, Liberty and the pursuit of Happiness." How, at any level, can a vision be followed through to realization and meaningful completion?

What is value stream breakdown?

Wikipedia defines value stream *mapping* as follows:

"Value-stream mapping, also known as 'material-and-information-flow mapping', is a Lean management method for analyzing the current state and designing a future state for the series of events that take a product or service from the beginning of the specific process until it reaches the customer."

Several global consulting firms have specialists working with value stream mapping. This method involves observing how an operational process is performed in an AS-IS state and then moving on to formulate how the operational process can be improved or replaced by a better option in a future TO-BE state. This is all good and can be hugely useful as the delta between AS-IS and TO-BE is manageable for the client organization. It is possible to gauge future changes in the company upfront and run qualified risk assessments on potential consequences before change takes place. This is a rather safe way to implement change in any organization.

The gap analysis also contributes to easier management of progress, measurement of deliverables, KPIs, and discrepancies according to plan. The difference between the AS-IS and TO-BE is a functional way to navigate static environments in a manageable way. Some may find my concern about this way of working with change exaggerated; still, at times I fear that when real change is needed, not enough new advances and developments will come out of such change projects where static landmarks and KPIs are applied. Disruptive solutions venture into the unknown. Defining the TO-BE in the beginning limits future destinations in terms of what can be understood and dealt with. Value stream mapping can be applied to work processes, production lines, and revenue streams, but to me, it is not innovative and will never bring any disruptive elements into any part of the process involved.

By not disrupting anything, the business model is barely affected, if at all, and life will continue close to what it was up until the change project for many. Focusing on static states is a good way to eliminate bottlenecks in any organization. Making modifications on a smaller scale will ensure that the company will never venture into any new territory. Value stream mapping is a good way to ensure secure and stable continuity for most in the organization. It can easily turn into a pat on the shoulder for management that they are doing 'operations in the right way'.

Obviously, it is not the aim or mission of every organization or business to be innovative. I have the personal impression that doing things LEAN is often portrayed as change for the better, while LEAN is about improvement. I claim executives around the world are doing great jobs at making their processes and organizations LEANER and more efficient while they actually claim to be innovative.

These two, improvement and disruption, I consider to be opposites and need to be recognized as such. One improves or enhances the status quo within certain limits, while the other disrupts, and perhaps even disturbs, the workings of human beings. One is continuing to play by the rules of the game, just playing the game better, while the other is changing the fundamental rules of the game. Sure, improvements can be innovative, but often disruption is much more so.

Given the context of value stream mapping, a new way of thinking is required to eliminate a great deal of process thinking. The intention is to move our minds straight to value creation without getting entangled in the process. Value stream breakdown, as opposed to value stream mapping, is all about starting with the end value in mind. Drilling down, beyond the effect of the use case, defines a potential tangible result in the form of a defined value. The idea is that, in the end, there can never be more than a handful of results that a commercial organization should strive for. My claim is that any end goal for a use case will ultimately look like one of the following operational KPIs:

- Financial benefit
  - Reduced or managed cost

- Quality
  - Improved or managed quality

- Efficiency
  - Improved or managed efficiency of the production line, or product output from the production line

Traditional project management has three overall measurement parameters that need to be kept under continuous control: time, cost, and quality. Operational, tangible KPIs in the realms of finance, quality, and efficiency will serve a similar function when developing use cases. Efficiency in a use case may point to the time vs. volume of a production line, or it may reflect the financial cost and production time vs. quality of a product. I like to think of these three overarching parameters as finance, quality, and efficiency. Comparing them to value parameter measurement tools such as time, cost, and quality, you can plan within given limits, yet the moment you make any changes to one or more of these three parameters, you will automatically impact the remaining KPIs.

If you decrease production costs, the quality of the product or efficiency of the production line may suffer. If you improve the quality of the product, it may take longer to produce, affecting the efficiency of the production line negatively, or you may drive the production cost up altogether. The space of possibility for creating value with a product is always within this continuous triangle. You can shift the three around actively or reactively, but you can never escape the product's end result, which is a result of choices, by factoring in any one or all of these three parameters. It is, of course, possible to optimize all three through careful planning or mere coincidence. Some refer to that sweet spot as instinctual or a result of years of experience. A LEAN project will typically work with optimizing the balance between these three parameters by focusing on the optimization of the processes applied.

Keep in mind that marketing and visibility of a product, when building a brand name, also make up the product, as the end game is still sales or a measurable financial benefit. The parameters of financial benefit, quality, and efficiency are as valid as ever when the internal effect of a use case raises sales. Also, if increased market trust in a given brand following a marketing campaign results in a greater market share, this is because a marketing campaign is a product in its own right, even when it is a supporting act to the core product.

While developing a framework of value stream breakdowns, I questioned whether I should separate out health, safety, security, and quality (HSSQ) as a separate area of value creation. I decided against it. Any organization may decide to work with HSSQ as an independent value parameter. The reason why I prefer not to include HSSQ as a separate currency in the value matrix is that compliance in the area is ultimately driven by the parameters of quality and finance. For instance, the market share of a company may suffer directly if it is not scoring as expected on the HSSQ charts. This can result in a dive in market trust for the given brand over time. A decrease in market share may follow as consumers become increasingly adept at picking up on the ethical shortcomings of production companies. What may seem like an emotional change in the marketplace will eventually be expressed in the form of financial results.

This way of thinking may also collapse the quality parameter into the financial realm. Changes in the quality of a product will be reflected in the sales and market share of the company. If one decides to collapse all value parameters into financial parameters, that could be a fully viable way to go about value measurement, as it is possible to measure a lot in the financial realm. Still, I think it makes sense to work with a more nuanced map with a small number of carefully chosen value parameters that truly matter for the business. This will create a space where workable levels of values can be dealt with in a productive way. This is also supported by classic logic and management theory. If a company or a team has too few KPIs, the financial side may end up governing it all. Meanwhile, the tangible effect of measures taken and use cases realized can become hard to measure in a sensible way. This is because every action will point towards that one financial goal without much possibility for nuanced KPI measurement.

For instance, if the aim of a company is to earn as much money as possible with a product, then every suggestion as to how to reach this goal is equally qualified. There will be no other value parameters to check and control beyond the all-encompassing financial value parameter. The value area will be defined at a too high level and clearly needs to be broken down in more tactical and operational detail. This breakdown of value parameters will have an effect on the quality or efficiency value of the company at some point.

The opposite of aiming for too few value KPIs would be a company working with 20+ KPIs for each department; believe me, I have seen this in real life several times. Leaders talk about each of the many KPIs as a strategy when it is clearly not. KPIs are mostly operational and owned by mid-management, sometimes without a solid foundation in the strategic aims of the company. This last point would reflect a company that has no clear direction and does not know where to aim as a whole.

Unfortunately, a lot of companies work at a heavily operationally detailed level where management fails to see or communicate well the direction of value creation for the organization as a whole. A common example of aiming for one high-level financial KPI would be a company that is out to get rich fast but cannot decide internally what their core product or market segment should be. This would, in fact, be a company with no clear strategic direction.

It is necessary to navigate the value creation of the entire organization skillfully. It is crucial to understand how the most important value-creation areas are expressed in strategy, tactics, and operations and how they are all related vertically.

There is one book that explains very well the application of logic when thinking and communicating in various layers: *The Pyramid Principle: Logic in Writing and Thinking*[17] by Barbara Minto. This is a textbook that is widely taught internally at most large management consulting firms. It basically elaborates on how to apply logic in thinking, writing, communication, and problem-solving. If you would like to explore the application of logic in business and communication, the nine dimensions already mentioned, with more details to come, can further your understanding of Minto's concepts.

I consider value stream breakdown to be a purposeful activity for teams working on use case development to focus on at an early stage of concept development. The moment a new use case has been formulated in more than three sentences, this work should be commenced. When an established real human problem is formulated and there are indications that the materials and data required are available, the first mapping of a breakdown structure of the expected values of the use case application should be done. Nobody can be expected to understand the exact value of a future use case. Still, it is of great importance at an early stage to have a clear idea about the value any given use case can be expected to provide.

When disruptive innovation takes place, the expected value may change in any direction during product development as something new and not yet experienced. Learning about the value creation of each innovative use case is an important process for the team involved. It could be that a use case shifts value from one area to another throughout the process. This is totally okay as long as the team tries to keep track of the type and amount of value that may be expected.

---

17   https://www.amazon.com/Pyramid-Principle-Logic-Writing-Thinking/dp/0273710516

One example of this is a use case of predictive maintenance on heavy production equipment. For example, one starts off with the KPI of reduced downtime in the production line due to a known bottleneck of a conveyor belt failing more often than should be expected. This use case with a KPI on efficiency is expected to have financial benefits because the factory will be able to increase product output per hour with the same production resources available. This is given that the conveyor belt downtime will be reduced. Then, when the use case is under development, another value emerges more strongly: the reduction of unwanted interruptions and events on the factory floor contributes to a safer work environment for onsite workers. It may turn out that in the long run, the value of reducing unwanted events, resulting in improved HSSQ levels, supersedes the value of increasing production line efficiency. Without knowing the exact outcome of the use case entirely upfront, there could be a shift in the prioritized area of value creation.

For many companies, it can prove hugely useful to do this value stream breakdown on a regular basis—perhaps even several times a year in some organizations. Not only to identify areas where new use cases will provide optimal value but also to monitor the value breakdown of already developed and implemented use cases.

It is not necessary for all to use the same value areas as described in this book. The matrix format may also be omitted. It is up to each organization and team to find out what type of value map provides the best accuracy considering the local conditions and context. It makes sense to start with the overall vision and mission of the company and then try to work with values that are as close to the core production line or product as possible. This is because the proximity to the core production line, or core product, is where the most value is likely to be found by any innovative use case.

I would encourage any worker, manager, or executive responsible for innovative solutions in the form of internal projects or product and market ownership to simply play around with the value stream breakdown model on page 104. One size may not fit all, but still, every organization needs to work with the *what* and the *how* as well as the overall expected effect. It can be both fun and eye-opening to work with internal value structures in this way.

It may be useful to keep track of how staff functions in the company also support important value streams. Often, staff functions like HR, accounting, and legal departments are considered some sort of satellite as they are not directly involved in the core production of products and services. Staff functions are still critical for the core production line to run smoothly. Let's look at the example of the housekeeping team in the office. Housekeeping is clearly a prerequisite for keeping the core production going, and many managers leave it like that, considering it an extra cost that is inevitable and required for the office to function. However, if one looks at the greater picture, one can easily fit cleaning services into the greater value stream breakdown picture of the company and try to articulate what tangible effects a clean office has. It may turn out that high-quality housekeeping is more important than onsite daycare for employees.

The cultural landscape changes across countries and business areas, so it can certainly be useful to work holistically with value streams. If nothing else, it will raise the awareness of all involved about how supportive functions in the form of internal capacities in the company add effect and value to core production. Also reminding everyone about what the core production line actually is. The practice of analyzing value streams may also lead to new observations and vantage points that have not been articulated earlier. I have seen many organizations where a high number of employees do not have the skills needed to understand the difference between internal capacities and the core product of the organization. Management often overlooks communicating this in a strong and clear way, assuming others see the inner workings of the company in the same way management does. It can also be assumed by leadership that making such distinctions may cause some employees or functions to be considered more important than others. Another presumption is that this information is too complicated for many employees to understand.

I believe that by articulating the type and form of value each part of the company produces, one can provide much-needed transparency about the value each individual, team, and department provides for the organization as a whole. The link to the core production line should be clear for all roles. Before minimizing staff functions, one needs to draw tangible lines as to how these functions provide value to the core production line or core product or service.

→ Clear ownership of value harvest
It cannot be overstated how important it is to place the ownership of the value to be harvested from each use case appropriately. For instance, it could be the CEO in the capacity of ownership of a strategic goal, or it could

be the HSSQ responsible for the operational facility. A product owner may need a long-term view of the financial target value for future sales to be successful with a new product. No matter where the ownership of the value harvest is placed, it is important to place it and put the responsibility where it belongs. It is clear for any startup or big conglomerate that market analysis reports are necessary. For any new product to find its way to a viable market share, and in any commercial venture, the development of new products and services needs to be market-driven. Yet, in the world of agile development, many individuals and departments churn out new proof of concepts and new products at a higher rate than ever before. It is important to ask how a clear enough direction may be achieved in new agile landscapes where good ideas flourish.

Independent of whether the internal vehicle of new product development is based on the application of dynamic agile methodologies or more traditional, static waterfall methods, management needs to keep a fixed eye on the role responsible internally for the value to be created by the new product or service. In this way, the focus will shift from the process itself to the expected output and value creation. It is crucial that there be tangible accountability for the expected value the new use case will provide. The use case is a consequence of a human problem, which implies that human responsibility needs to be placed on a business level. It is of less importance whether the development process is agile or traditional waterfall-based, as long as a real person is responsible for the outcome. Someone beyond the CEO in the organization should be appointed to this kind of KPI directly in the role description and be measured on it by management, or in some organizations by HR. It may be a product owner, an account manager, a market director, or someone else, depending on the area of business and the internal operations of the company. The most important thing is simply that the responsibility is placed somewhere real, and that ownership is not diluted or shared in several pieces.

It is also important that the mandate to influence output or value creation follow the responsibility of the value harvest. If the responsibility is placed on a team, the responsibility is already starting to dissolve, as any shared product ownership often dissolves individual accountability. A leader role needs to be assigned, as naming a committee may not provide the same clarity and direction. The book *The 7 Habits of Highly Effective People*[18] by Steven Covey describes very well the relationship between the circle of

---

18   https://en.wikipedia.org/wiki/The_7_Habits_of_Highly_Effective_People

responsibility and the circle of influence. When these two circles are not aligned in a role, the owner of the role may be challenged.

Organizations where each individual has more than one area of responsibility are often referred to as *matrix organizations*. This is an organizational structure in which employees have more than one line of reporting managers, which means each role reports to more than one boss. There is a shared responsibility for most deliverables. For instance, many roles in an organization require employees to take part in both project and line activities. Matrix organizations work well at keeping the status quo and keeping organizational and operational solidity in place, while it is immensely challenging to come up with any matrix organization that is innovative. In short, shared responsibility usually hampers progress. Another downside of matrix organizations is that the robustness of deliverables suffers as nobody, in particular, becomes responsible for outcomes beyond top management.

In most organizations, it makes sense to align the responsibility of value harvesting vertically. The executive-level role may be responsible for the strategic goal, the all-over effect, or a financial goal. Mid-management may be responsible for the tactical 'how-to' plan and output in the form of monitoring measurable output as a tangible effect. Production staff may be measured on KPIs like operational volumes and compliance to keep measurable output within the required value span.

Every use case in a larger organization should be reflected in the strategic, tactical, and operational KPIs of the different levels of the organization.

Working with a hierarchical structure of how operational KPIs underpin effects and ultimately business strategy, both bottom-up and top-down, management can ensure that all use cases and KPIs of the organization actually underpin a shared strategy. If analysis of any of the vertical levels show that a use case does not fit the current strategy, tactics, or KPIs for operations, it may not be completely wrong, but it makes sense to ask questions about the proposed value of the use case and the ownership and plan for value realization. When value charts are aligned and the use case is included, one knows there are good chances the use case is valid. In addition, it becomes easier to steer and tune the use case in the development phase.

→ The weighting of the potential value
If there is any further need to weigh different value parameters against each other, there are many good ways to do this. For example, through

portfolio management of projects or prioritizing incentives. Consulting firms often work out a risk analysis based on the probability and impact of a problem. Risk management can, in some cases, be applied in a reverse process where a similar consequence analysis can be created. Based on the probability of consequences and impact given when a use case is *not* developed. This may sound like an awkward way to back into any value description, yet by applying methods, the chains of reason will be made visible and can be documented and discussed.

Any piece of documentation where logic is applied to weigh innovation and use cases against each other can be far more useful than an upfront subjective weighing process. Reason is king. We are still dealing with new and often unknown territories. I will encourage a playful approach at the drawing board stage to find out what parameters and logic your organization and business will base its innovation on.

My preferred approach is to be more play-like in the early phases of the creative process. It is paramount to create the space needed in the organization for exploring different value models. It is not necessary to be original; one can easily create the same model as a competing company in the market. But, when innovating, it is crucial to investigate internally and ask if every stone has been turned when trying out value weighting models. This is an area where years of experience and seniority are easily outwitted by younger resources, as creativity contributes to success. Organizations that are open-minded and share a culture of accepting both trial and failure from their employees may fare much better at this task than authoritarian and more conformist organizations.

Another example of how to articulate the expected value of a future use case would be to estimate ratios. Explore the original human problem versus the effort to develop and implement the use case before gauging the impact of the solution the use case offers. Juxtaposing these three parameters will provide an initial overview of what effort will provide the best ROI from the given use case:

Original human problem

vs.

The effort to develop and implement the use case

vs.

Expected impact of solution offered by the use case

The original human problem needs to be important enough to provide real value when it is solved. Still, the effort to develop and implement the use case should not be overwhelming compared to the expected impact and value of the use case. There may be valid reasons for developing a use case. Also, it may not seem like a good decision to do so at first glance. This, in turn, demands an explanation and a weighting of effort versus value for the use case. If the main reason to develop the use case is outside the greater triangle of *problem, effort, and impact*, then high-quality communication will be needed across various stakeholders for the development and implementation to gain the momentum needed.

4. SKILLSETS OF STAKEHOLDERS

I believe the digital skillset of the stakeholders may be the most crucial reality check for any innovative use case, following the attention to the areas of problem, data, and value. If the organization building the product or the consumer market does not understand the value to be created well enough, then the use case will simply not succeed. The tech revolution does not happen when innovative tech initially is put out in the market. The revolution happens when there is a shared understanding between the organization building the product and the average consumer of why the product is needed.

Once more, I will use the example of smartphones. It was not until a certain mass of consumers had developed the skill to use apps for personal needs that the smartphone really gained traction in the market. At the same time, the producers of the first successful smartphones had to hire forward-leaning, tech-savvy developers to get the product they really wanted ready for the market. The designers of the first successful smartphones that captured major parts of the mobile phone market understood that easy access to apps and a fast understanding of their functionality were essential parts of a successful launch. The accessibility of the user interface (UX) was crucial for the market share to grow fast enough for smartphones to succeed.

I will share a consulting experience I had where the internal stakeholders overlooked a vital skill set to create a potentially valuable use case. My project was to implement software asset life cycle management for Software as a Service (SaaS) products in a large corporation. In short, my job was to ensure that all software was appropriately licensed and that valid contracts were in place. My use case was to provide a holistic, top-down governance structure. This would ensure that all contracted software used to provide the SaaS products would be bundled and managed in a contract portfolio tool within the organization. By collecting licensing data in a structured, top-down way, my hypothesis included a 30% reduction in licensing fees company-wide. The idea was that the business side could optimize licensing of software packages, procurement could better negotiate existing and new licenses, and the company could eliminate unneeded licenses.

An early step was to engage with the chief software product architect of the company. After a brief conversation, I realized that the architect had no knowledge or understanding of governing frameworks or best practices in the realm of company governance. I tried to explain the situation, but my use case fell flat without the engagement of this one important stakeholder. My project was subsequently canceled. There was no ownership of a potential 30% cut in licensing fees connected with any particular role in the company, including the chief software product architect. The relevant role holder could not be held accountable for the effect of optimizing an enterprise-wide value chain.

The architect was key to obtaining the data needed for this use case, but as the reward was not visible to this person, there was no motivation to collect the relevant data.

The use case prioritized by the IT department the following quarter was an improved automated code review tool for the chief software product architect and development team. This was not necessarily a bad thing in itself, but I never observed anyone in the IT department show a strong understanding of the fundamental difference between the internal capacity they were investing in and the product portfolio. There was no focus on discerning between use cases that were close to or more peripheral to the core product.

It can be argued that both use cases in question were internal capacities. Still, I believe it would have been useful to weigh them against each other and in proximity to the core product. If a value stream breakdown had been done, one could visualize how the effect of the investment on the core product through the raised quality of corrected code would probably be a smaller win than the optimized pricing of the software components of the SaaS packages. Such a reduction in product costs could substantially reduce the market price of the SaaS product offering. In the end, it was a lack of knowledge and shared understanding that caused the company to miss this opportunity.

Another and perhaps more universally pressing example of where competence is needed is the digitalization of national infrastructures, such as national railways. For more than a century, national rail companies have relied on mainly analog skillsets when maintaining rail tracks. A rail switch has historically required mechanical understanding and perhaps electrical skills to function. By introducing digitized rail systems, there is a big shift towards digital skills needed in the rail workforce. Electrical switchboards have been replaced by server rooms, and manual relays in the track have been replaced by digital motorized ones. Where rail technicians used to get by with a toolbox full of manual tools like pliers and crowbars, it is now expected that server upgrades are performed in the server rooms, often by the same employees. Rail technicians with decades of experience are sent to training courses for new types of rail relays. There, they are expected to learn advanced server settings, while they have never before been expected to use any form of PC or other digital tools in their role. The digital shift is often applauded in public, while it puts a strain on many internal resources to acquire an entirely new level of digital skills to keep delivering the product and service quality expected by the end-user.

I have observed that the private use of digital tools, like the smartphone, might be the greatest enabler for digitizing entire industries. I have heard it said so many times that older employees make up the biggest liability when it comes to updating skills in the digital area. My experience does not confirm this image. In training sessions, I have repeatedly experienced that the grandparents in the classroom are the most concerned about not having the basic skills required for the new digital tools on offer. More often than not, when getting into the practice part of the training, the very same grandparents lighten up when they realize that what they are expected to do is not much harder than opening a Skype session with their grandkids. The personal qualities of openness and curiosity mean a lot more than age when it comes to the ability to acquire new digital skills in changing professions.

However, the degree of digital competence needed varies greatly between organizations and business areas. I observe that the greater challenge is often for non-digital professions to transform into highly digitalized professions. The example of rail technicians demonstrates this. Domain experts who already include some PC utilization during a workday are often less challenged by the introduction of new digital interfaces, simply because the new digital interfaces are tailored for easy user access. Domain experts already working digitally experience an adjustment in their digital work process, while analog professions experience an entire shift from an analog sphere to a digital one.

This all may seem heartbreakingly unfair, yet I believe the bottom line is that true domain expertise in human form will never be superfluous in the face of digitalization. The less specialized worker who has long postponed digitalization is far more at risk of being excluded from a current role by new technology replacing humans.

The general attitude towards using new technology and learning new digital skills is more important than a deep level of technical understanding of the use case itself. I have seen top management break out of the digitalization pace of their organization because he or she feels personally digitally weak. When one or more of the stakeholders in the organization are resistant to the pace of digitalization, that can be enough for the entire change process towards new technology to slow down. It is simply the willingness to be open and interested and to try to understand a wider perspective of the organization's purpose that matters most. The managers that find it hard to hire people more skilled than themselves are the ones that may fare the worst in digital transformation.

Organizational culture for learning and taking risks is easily a far more decisive factor in successful innovative use case development than the age of any product manager. When that is said, it is humbling to see the digital skills of recent graduates and how digital knowledge is increasingly a fresh commodity. This must be renewed faster than ever for companies to keep up with their markets.

In the past, a traditionalist conservative manager would often require a young graduate to do years of supportive functions before he or she was allowed a role with real impact. Today, the young graduate will increasingly walk away from such jobs as he or she understands that fresh digital skills need to be applied quickly so that their knowledge is not wasted. Without applying their fresh knowledge, the graduate is likely to lag in the job market as their skills expire.

I believe most organizations require a well-considered balance of established and new skills, as static and dynamic knowledge complement each other.

Experienced employees can provide insights and static knowledge that takes years to accumulate, while younger employees can often offer more dynamic observations and creativity that may be overlooked. While years of experience is a great asset, younger personnel have fresh skills and are eager to put them to use. In my vision of a perfect world, there is no either-or between the two but rather a wish to have it all in a complementary fashion where synergies and co-creation are prioritized.

To sum it up, for new and innovative use cases to succeed, I believe an organizational culture is required where digital skills are built and maintained in parallel with putting fresh skills cleverly to use. If too much pride is put in past successes and experiences while fresh skills are not put to optimal use, the culture of stagnation is bound to hamper the company. Not every company needs to be innovative, but if innovation is a goal in itself or required by a changing market, then the skills of many stakeholders need to be aligned and digitized accordingly.

5. PROCESS
A famous quote often attributed to Albert Einstein goes as follows:

"The definition of insanity is doing the same thing over and over again, but expecting different results."

In other words, if you want different results, you will have to try different approaches.

Besides my strong focus on value creation, I believe it is important to know where you are in the process. Recognizing the very process you are in is crucial. When working with a new use case, there is an overwhelming chance that you will affect existing processes in the organization. If no processes are affected, chances are that the use case may not be very impactful.

It can be a success criterion to keep track of how a new use case affects processes. The more a new use case is about building internal capability, the more it is likely to change the way people work. The more a new use case is about revolutionizing a product or service or changing a business model or market share, the more the organization needs to change its existing production or market processes to reach the goal.

The equation is simple: Many new things will come out of doing things in a novel way. The opposite of this would be to try to create something new while doing things the same way as in the past. If the approach is not changed, chances are that the outcome will be similar to earlier results.

Some companies introduce IoT and ML in their organization by introducing chatbots in their customer service department. This is seen as a relatively easy entry point to new technologies, often in the form of RPA. The disruptive part of introducing chatbots is that a resource-consuming work process traditionally performed by support staff is eliminated. This is beyond process improvement. When introducing a chatbot, many companies will reduce their need for human frontline support by more than 50%. Still, the reward of introducing chatbots is not affecting the end product, the market share, or the core production process. It is simply eliminating the need for a human workforce in the process. RPA takes pretty much the same steps the human service agent would take during frontline support and replaces them with a digitized process, including a digital UX for the consumer.

The introduction of chatbots can be seen as a good place to start when introducing innovative use cases. The truth is that while it can be a good way to optimize operational costs internally, the introduction of RPA hardly affects anything else. The quality of the service provided by a chatbot may be improved compared to the human service formerly provided, or it may not. That depends on the quality of either.

It is a good idea to take the time to observe and measure the process maturity of the organization when it comes to creating value from the introduction of new technology. New use cases can be applied to internal capabilities, to product and service development, or to both. A production company typically focuses on building internal capabilities first, for instance by introducing chatbots, and then creates a base from which it feels more secure to venture forward to new use cases in the product sphere. Scaling digitalization with a low number of use cases in parallel can be the traditional path to getting closer to the core production line or core product. That is scaling from peripheral functions to increasingly more important functions.

There is nothing holding a company back from immediately aiming at the most valuable use cases, closer to the core production line and product offering. It is simply important to understand where one is in the process landscape when creating use cases. It is not necessarily wrong to develop use cases aiming at processes far from the core production process or core product. But it is important to understand that the value of these use cases would often be lower than use cases developed in direct proximity to the core product or core production line. In other words, there may be valuable lessons to be learned in every part of the organization through innovation, but remain vigilant where your most value-returning use cases may be found.

→ First step: asset management and belonging datasets

Many production companies start their development of use cases by applying old datasets to resolve known problems in the area of asset management. This can be a good step towards securing and optimizing the production line. Examples here would be use cases involving predictive maintenance of production equipment, innovative data models for risk analysis, and real-time video surveillance of heavy assets in the production line. This would include detection, recognition, and possibly correction of anomalies.

→ Second step: process information

When this first step of utilizing datasets around production infrastructure is successful, the natural maturing of adding process information to the equipment and operational datasets often proves timely. The better the fidelity of the datasets regarding asset management, the more opportunity there is to succeed in improving or disrupting processes. This includes access to correct information about production equipment and connected infrastructure. It is usually a prerequisite that the organization has insight into its production environment and related assets before changing the work processes.

A classic example would be the use case of introducing mobile digital interfaces for production floor operators to monitor production equipment. In that way, the operator will reduce the need to actually be present in different places on the production floor while taking down status and measurements from the actual production assets. Time saved can be spent in one place, monitoring the overall status and measurements digitally. Working from a higher vantage point of information is often a benefit. This reduces the need for the operator to move around on the production floor and perhaps even the need to be present on the production floor.

To be able to do this successfully, it is necessary to make the required information about production infrastructure available digitally. Additionally, it is necessary to make sure the relevant datasets available have sufficient fidelity. If the quality of the datasets is not good enough, the operator will likely have to re-enter the work floor and check status and measurements manually once more, as he or she cannot trust the digitized data provided.

Obviously, there may be many times when work processes can be altered or eliminated without the introduction of datasets or any other new technology. The innovation rate can still be great without any other input other than changes and disruptions to the work process itself. The vantage point presented shows how new technology in the form of new datasets is an enabler for innovation. Especially in the area of work processes and other processes in any organization. The leverage on processes that new datasets open up can easily be a huge advantage in how the entire organization works.

Here is an example of how a process not related to the workforce can be hugely improved: Imagine if the procurement department had insight into what make of production equipment would be the most reliable over its lifetime. If benchmarks on productivity and downtime could be predicted for each heavy asset and individual production equipment, this would provide important steering information for the finance department regarding future maintenance and procurement of new production equipment. This would make for a big shift in how the procurement process would become more complex with the added parameters of ROI besides the existing technical requirements, functional requirements, price, and quality parameters usually in use for the procurement process.

This is often an easy use case to develop; all it takes is a business intelligence dashboard where innovative constellations of enterprise-wide data and advanced statistics, perhaps with additional ML functionality, are made available for the executive management. In this case, the innovative factor would be the constellation of operational data and heavy asset data, together with the financial and procurement data.

→ Third step: getting closer to the core production line
If use cases in the areas of assets and processes are well established, it makes sense to pursue the search for the most valuable use cases in the core production line or in the core product itself. Insights from heavy asset management and processes in the organization are often well suited to build a foundation upon which valuable use cases in the production line can be addressed. It is, of course, possible to start working on use

cases in the core production line right away, yet for some, it turns out that checking the maturity of heavy asset management and processes in the organization is worthwhile. This is because many use cases in the core production line will rely on datasets that affect heavy asset management, work processes, and supportive processes before they can provide value in the core production line. I will be the first to say that this is not an absolute rule, yet I will provide a couple of examples of how this can work.

Imagine a large-scale clothing production company that would like to optimize the use of raw materials in the production line. The use case is to optimize the utilization of raw materials in a way that both reduces waste and improves the quality of the product. It is possible to analyze the amount, type, and visual patterns of fabrics and match them with how robot sewing machines best make use of each roll of fabric to create the optimal number of shirts with the correct patterned look. In this way, the cost of fabric per shirt is reduced to a minimum in a way that humans most likely would not be able to match. It is important to have a deep understanding of how the production equipment works and which parameters can be used with it. In addition, a good understanding of the human interaction with the production line for the desired outcome of patterns in shirts is required to be able to get the optimal result. There would be no use for a higher number of shirts per roll if the patterns were all placed erratically and the shirts did not look as expected.

In this use case, domain expertise in a digital format matters. It would be necessary to combine tailoring expertise as a process parameter with the optimization of the robot sewing machine to make this a successful endeavor. Insight as to how the production equipment works is needed in conjunction with domain expertise.

The heavy asset industry today is experiencing a huge shift towards the software industry. Where heavy assets used to be mostly a mechanical business, it is now becoming more common to add software to the offering. Over the last decades, unique serial numbers have become increasingly common on heavy equipment and machinery in a variety of industries, as well as on smaller parts making up assets. The capacity to track production equipment digitally has opened opportunities for applying new and innovative use cases, from optimization of maintenance cycles on production equipment to fully operational digital twins encompassing entire installations and production sites.

According to Wikipedia, a digital twin is a virtual representation that serves as the real-time digital counterpart of a physical object or process. I believe it can also refer to any virtual (or digital) representation of a physical entity.

→ Fourth step: aiming to go exponential with the product

The first three steps mentioned are often about adding internal capabilities to the company in various forms. This is all great, but most internal capabilities will never deliver close to the value that an improvement to the product itself can provide. This is why moving innovation into the product itself can provide exponential value compared to any internal capability. Sure enough, many companies invest more in product development than in their internal IT department, and they are often right to do so. When introducing new datasets, as mentioned above, this difference may be erased in a way that was not possible before. The exploration of new data from both inside the company and outside makes a range of new use cases possible, and for most companies, there are few, if any, other places besides the product itself that can provide the highest value.

In some businesses, it is challenging, or not possible at all, to influence the product directly with innovation, while in other areas, product innovation is the only thing that matters. For instance, oil-producing companies would give a lot to be able to improve the quality of the oil produced. As this is a challenge at an early stage of the product life cycle, oil exploration companies are focusing on how much oil they can produce and at what cost over a given time. This does not mean that the quality of the oil cannot, and is not, improved during the production process. It just seems that improving the quality of the production line is a more accessible option in many cases.

An example of a product that can be influenced by new datasets would be networks for mobile phone users. By adding algorithms to improved datasets on geographical coverage, more targeted service development can take place in areas where the most end-users will benefit from improved coverage. The use case is that improved datasets on mobile network coverage quality will enable improved service for the highest number of end-users, while the reinvestment will remain as low as possible as recently discovered bottlenecks can be targeted. This use case would both enhance and optimize existing product and service offerings, and it would open opportunities for developing new service offerings for new geographic market segments. For instance, improving app offerings such as adding GPS detail and increasing functionality in remote areas. It may not sound crucial, but personally, I know that an improved map navigation tool for the less traveled parts of the Norwegian natural parks on my smartphone would quickly have me convinced to choose one operator over another.

Another example of a use case affecting the product would be a sawmill where the production manager would like to better optimize the utilization of different types of wood going into the mill so that a greater differentiation of raw materials can be applied directly in the production process. The use case would be to optimize the utilization of logs going into the sawmill based on quality criteria. One can apply an additional 3D scan of each log going into the mill so that the thickness and type of material produced will be based on the thickness and physical shape of each log. It would make sense to use bigger and straighter logs for thicker and longer planks, while smaller and more crooked logs may suit better for small furniture-making with shorter planks. If this use case is applied skillfully, the new dataset of 3D images may enable each log to be tagged to a finished product before it meets the saw in the production line. One is looking at a specific bottleneck regarding the quality of the product itself in the core production line. Instead of improving or disrupting a greater part of the process, one looks specifically at one pain point in the entire value chain. This improves the quality of the product directly instead of optimizing any parameters along the core process of production.

Whenever a business can improve a product substantially, a new landscape emerges that should demand careful consideration from the executive management and often from the board too. The reason is that improved products have the potential to shift business models significantly, not always in an exclusively positive way. A hypothetical example could be a building entrepreneur: if the building process moved entirely from a drawing board to a fully digitized 3D AutoCAD program, the time span of the planning process could potentially be cut by a fraction. Given that the improvement in the planned product is also revolutionary due to enhanced accuracy and efficiency of floor planning, it is probable that the company will be out of profitable work within a couple of years, given that their competitors have caught up on the concept and followed suit in the market. It is important to find a sweet spot between innovation rate and profitability when it comes to how products, and hence markets, are affected by innovation.

Most of us have heard about how Kodak failed to innovate and follow up on digital use cases for product development until they reached the point where they had to close their existing business. A few are less familiar with the current conundrum of many service companies where service is the core product. They are innovating their way out of current markets by reducing the hours spent on each task due to efficient digitalization. Any business supplying services and charging customers on a time and materials basis will need to take care not to become too efficient when making shifts to how they work. They need to pay close attention to their business models and innovate on them first. Then they can build capacity according to time and materials required rather than end up with empty ordering books because service contracts were finished too efficiently for their own good. If the product, or service in this last-mentioned example, is getting too cheap and the competitors in the market are forced to follow due to market prices being cut again and again, the company will need to navigate yet uncharted waters in finding out how to make their specific business model work.

Product innovation has the power of dynamite, and it requires a certain amount of careful consideration and risk management to ensure that it supports the company's strategy in a fruitful way, both in the short-term and the long-term. The alternative is that the product, service, or even the market may be disrupted in a way that challenges the organization to cannibalize itself unless it manages to change its organization on a large scale or replace its business model swiftly.

6. SCALABILITY
Before the development of a use case starts, there should be a clear point of view about the possibility of future scaling of the specific use case. There will be situations where a single-use case with a single implementation or single instance will create enough value for it to be developed. In the majority of use cases that provide the most value in the long run, scalability is a success factor.

An example of horizontal scalability would be the Johnson Space Center in Houston, Texas, which manages flight control for America's human space program. This is one cohesive entity that monitors and controls the International Space Station. As there is only one International Space Station to be monitored, the scalability lies in extending datasets horizontally to be monitored, not by replicating instances of space stations.

By scalability, I refer to the possibility of extending the use case in the same or similar scenarios several times, or the opportunity to scale up the way the use case is applied in the first place. I like to think of scalability as a set of parameters that follow certain principles. Often in this process, new data, or datasets, are added to an instance of the use case, or a company extends the application area of a use case.

Often, a use case stands out immediately because it is so clear what kind and what scale of value it will provide. When this point of view is clear, it makes sense to backtrack to the efficiency and optimization of the given parameters in the use case to analyze *why* a certain value is to be expected. This is where scalability enters the spotlight. We are once again encountering the juxtaposed triangle in the measurement of efficiency, optimization, and value. At least one of these three parameters needs to be quite convincing for the use case to be developed. If parameters indicating the value of the use case are not within a given scope, the value cannot be predicted to be high enough for the development of the use case to take place. Are there any recognizable factors in the parameters that make it easier to recognize if the use case is scalable (or replicable) or not? The good news is that I believe there are.

I have observed that the term 'scalability' is often applied to both scalable and replicable use cases. I prefer to differentiate between the two, as the nuances between them articulate the nature of the future growth of the use case.

A use case that is less scalable and more replicable is the application of a rich 3D digital twin. For the sake of the example, let's use a 3D digital twin of an offshore oil rig containing operational data. There may be some clever ways and best practices to efficiently build an extensive 3D digital twin. However, the fact remains that connecting each detailed object contained in a unique 3D model is an elaborate process. Best practices and standards for introducing data ontologies do not eliminate the fact that this can be a large amount of work. In the future, I would expect new methods and tools to make the job far easier. The consequence of the extensive manual workload is that the use case is not very scalable. Uniqueness in models has historically provided less opportunity for automation of data mapping.

A 3D digital twin of almost any installation can be hugely useful when it comes to enhancing human understanding of relationships and perspectives among various elements and parameters. The time and resources required to build a complex, layered 3D digital twin have long been prohibitive. Since new and better modeling tools were made available in recent years, more industrial business areas have ventured into this space of development. In many cases, it may still take months, or even years, to build a complete 3D digital twin of an operational facility. Without the one-to-one matching of elements, parameters, and processes in the model, the value of such a 3D digital twin may be limited. Data fidelity is crucial.

Each oil rig is built in a unique way, so there is no easy fix to replicate 3D digital twins of such installations globally. That said, when a rich and accurate 3D digital twin is built and made available, it can provide great value as it can relate all items, data points, systems, and operational data. This is an ideal resource for developing numerous further use cases for the specific installation in question as well as for the entire industry.

When there is no standard heavy asset in an industry or when the production line is unique and has a large number of data layers in some form, it can be labor-intensive to build an encompassing use case. The best approach is to think about simplicity and parameters first. That often makes a use case more scalable. Look for data that is shared, or at least understood, across the enterprise. When working with a smaller part of a large unit, bottleneck problems can be defined and resolved by far more accessible use cases than a complex enterprise-wide approach to data.

7. REPLICABILITY
By replicability, I refer to the possibility of re-applying the use case in the same or similar scenarios several times.

A common use case that is universal and replicable can be found in logistics. How to optimize the boxes or parcels stacked in a shipping container is a task that has evolved into an entire profession. Some basic parameters here are the shape and volume of boxes, the profit margin of each box to be shipped, and the space available for stacking in the container. Together, these parameters make it possible to optimize the income generated for each container based on the boxes or parcels available for each transport lag. Because the parameters are universal and the equation between the parameters is universal, the use case is globally replicable and scalable. The parameters and data layers of this use case are identical across facilities, nations, and continents. Of course, variations in circumstances may occur, yet the fundamentals are similar whether one transports frozen goods or shoes.

Let's also look at one of the use cases already discussed: the 3D scan of logs going into a sawmill so that the use of each log is optimized in production. This is optimizing the use of resources. The use case can easily be replicated and installed on a large number of sawmills globally. There may be variations between different types of trees used for logging and various product requirements. For instance, the sawmill may produce material for house paneling or furniture. Still, the circumstances of the use case are general and can be re-applied a high number of times.

When looking for scalable use cases, it makes sense to focus on a few select parameters that are tangible and measurable. It should be clear how these parameters are applied in an equation that results in a value that is measurable and important. It may be an exaggeration to say that complex use cases are less valuable, while they are most often unique and take more time and resources to develop than the simpler ones. An easily shared understanding of the use case and accessible data should never be underestimated.

TAKE AWAY ON SCALABILITY AND REPLICABILITY
A checkpoint for scalability is to make sure that the applied parameters are actually providing value. The value parameters need to be tangible and measurable. If they cannot be measured in an accessible way, it will be hard to assess any value the use case provides. If the value of the use case cannot be properly measured in some form, then the question of scalability remains. The why will also remain unanswered.

A checkpoint for replicability is the equation of the parameters involved. If they are static and valid independent of scale and sometimes business areas, it indicates that the use case can be repeated and replicated.

You may start to observe that replicable use cases are often the ones that are based on simple parameters, carefully chosen for their ability to bring specific value. It is true that without the necessary data available, there will be no use case. Still, I consider the value parameter to be the most important. If the value is not real, then there is no reason for the use case to exist.

I once received the suggestion of building an e-shop with integrated 3D models and data-rich digital twins of the online product offerings. At the time, it sounded very alluring for the sales department to include a high-tech presentation of each product. The details of the product would be more visually accessible, and for the client, it would be fun and interesting to browse and observe the unique product details in 3D models. My recommendation was against it. The idea was endearing, but in this specific case, I could not see how the datasets for each product would provide any real value to the customer beyond the value already present in the existing product documentation. The product presentation would be more attractive, and the instant understanding of how each product was visually unique would bring a more intuitive understanding of the entire product to the customer. But I did not believe that the investment in building new 3D digital twins of all products, beyond the simplified 3D models already available, would be worth the investment.

I kept asking rhetorically what the most important interest of the end customer was. My hypothesis was that the visualization of the product purely for sales purposes would not be the best available use case at the time. An end customer intending to invest heavily in a piece of heavy machinery would, in my opinion, take the time to evaluate the technical specifications in an Excel document and not let the buying decision lean on an impressive product presentation. We never found out as we explored other use cases where enriched 3D models were applied. A takeaway here is to observe whether the use case is close to the core product or if data enrichment and contextualization are limited to supportive acts in the organization. Sales are crucial, yet the value of the use case would potentially be higher when closer to the core product.

If you have a use case and you cannot easily explain why and how it is scalable or replicable with existing parameters, then you may want to keep searching for a simpler application of another use case involving the same data sources. This is because simplicity in itself often makes a use case and its potential value easier to communicate and convey.

A wise man once shared an important insight with me. When working with object-oriented software, any kind of scaling you cannot do in real life but is possible in the cyber realm can potentially provide great value. One example is weather modelling. If a simulation is accelerated or decelerated substantially, or if a timeline is reduced or enlarged sufficiently, valuable insights can be found in spaces that the human eye has not seen before. For instance, climatic models would not have provided as much value if their time span did not extend beyond 100 years. Additionally, by running a 10,000,000-year simulation, one can possibly assess the accuracy of the model in several ways.

8. VISIBILITY

In other parts of this book, potential value creation is defined through the lenses of financial benefit, quality, and efficiency. Yet, there is another dimension encompassing all three that may be useful to explore before deciding upon the time and effort to be spent on developing a use case. Visibility may not be a value in itself. It can be challenging, especially up front, to gauge the potential value that visibility or exposure may provide. Sometimes a use case may not be seen as particularly valuable in the most obvious ways of measurement. Still, one can somehow see that it is important to develop the use case without being able to explain exactly why within existing frameworks of operations.

Often, external factors play a role, like an image or influence in the marketplace. Profiling of technical advances or simply the conviction among stakeholders that the use case is feasible and therefore should be developed and realized. When the reason a use case should be developed does not fall within the parameters of operations, it may be productive to ask whether the use case is valuable due to any visibility it has the potential to create.

When enriched digital twins of installations in the oil and gas industry were first made, the learning curves were steep before truly valuable use cases were developed. The main reason for many operators in the business to endeavor to build a digital twin was that it was perceived as a necessary thing to do. Younger, competing companies would increasingly base their entire operations on digital models. From there, entire operational landscapes would evolve around a *single digital enterprise model*. This startled many traditional actors in the market, who decided they needed to follow. Sometimes without even knowing exactly why.

Faith provides part of the motivation to push enriched digital twins forward. Sometimes early use cases in digital transformations are not successful because a clear direction for value creation has not yet been explored. At times, there has been no clear reason why a company should develop enriched digital twins, except a strong and shared understanding among leadership that it is the right thing to do. Sometimes, the underlying reason is that the leadership prefers not to be seen as the market contender that does not venture out on the exploratory path of using enriched digital twins. Image and branding mean a lot, and the place in the spotlight as a forward-leaning technology enterprise often feels like a critical factor to keep up any potential market shares. In other words, the psychology of self-image plays a major role.

More often than not, there is a conscious market strategy driving the development of enriched digital twins. Other times, it is internal operations driving the need, and that can pave the way for more mature use cases later. The cases I am focusing on here are the ones where visibility is the winning factor for spending resources on developing complex technology, often before the maturity of truly valuable use cases are in place. The reasons for leadership wanting visibility may be valid or not. Often, it is the job of the marketing department to decide.

In parallel, there are often operational domain experts that drive the development of complex use cases, sometimes without detailed consideration of the true value of the final product. It feels fun and exciting to develop the use case, simply because there is an opportunity to do so. In the end, the developer can showcase the use case triumphantly and express, "I made this super cool thing!" A few months later, the excitement may have calmed as the solution fizzles when it does not provide measurable value, or the solution is not well maintained and never reaches full operational implementation or any market.

Both leadership and savvy tech domain workers may create use cases for the sake of visibility. It can be a strategic decision to do so, to carve out space for innovation internally, or to choose this visibility as a market strategy. The importance of visibility in use cases should not be underestimated. Not strategically, nor for the potential market influence, nor as an internal motivator for innovation. The validity of visibility should be gauged by the leadership of any enterprise undertaking innovation. If nothing else, then at least understand the internal drivers for innovation in the organization better.

Sometimes the situation may be the other way around: there is a need to keep use cases from being visible. An example of this would be a successful use case improving the quality of a product. The beauty industry may have a high ratio of such low-visibility use cases. Not many end-users would like to know the secrets of the recipe, but they are willing to purchase a product based on either a real improvement in the quality of the product or because of the influence a targeted marketing campaign provides.

An analog use case that could easily be one of the simplest use cases ever developed is the optimization (in this case, maximization) of the hole in the tube of toothpaste. The unconfirmed story goes that an inventor contacted Colgate with the offer to share an insight into product development that he claimed would raise their sales volume of toothpaste significantly. He kindly requested $10,000,000 up front for his idea. After some contemplation, Colgate accepted the offer and paid the man $10,000,000. His tip: "Make the hole bigger!" Of course, he understood that the width of the bristles of each toothbrush would be static, while many users would apply toothpaste along the length of the brush, not looking at the thickness of the paste distributed. He got his ten million dollars, and Colgate got their increased sales as promised. The idea that this is a use case is unknown to most, but it makes the consumption by the end-user more efficient (or more wasteful). We may all use a bit more toothpaste every time we brush our teeth because of it.

Altogether, the visibility of use cases constitutes a complex and large landscape. The vantage point of required visibility can at times be a subjective opinion. In the end, visibility still crystallizes down to measurable value creation, while the variety of value and for whom it is created make up a complex weave. Usually, some form of visibility from the use case is clearly desired, while in some special cases, visibility is not even wanted. The defense sector is an area where visibility of digital use cases is often avoided.

9. DEVELOPMENT REQUIRED

The amount of development required to build a full-scale use case should at least be roughly estimated before a prototype is developed. It may be costly and time-consuming to build an exact estimate before prototyping and scaling are initiated, but it still makes sense to keep cost and time in check before starting the technical development. A good enough rule of thumb for many would be to keep a short, documented estimate of hours and costs updated at regular intervals throughout the phases of planning and development.

Any traditional project management methodology will proclaim a profound need to keep tight control of estimates and costs throughout any project. As use case development is a far more agile activity than most projects, it does not make sense to spend too much time on estimations before starting development. 'Fail fast' is an important motto of agile methodologies. If you look it up online, you will find many books on the topic. When working with use case development, it is crucial to be able to pivot when necessary.

Keep steering while making smaller, necessary decisions along the way, and aim towards constantly tuning cost estimations instead of setting aside a greater amount of resources and then figuring out what should be built.

When estimating the development required to build a use case, it is useful to make statements as to how much resources and time one *believes* will be used and not try to formulate the exact number of resources and time one *thinks* will be used. This shift in vantage point towards the development of solutions may be a leap of trust for many deeply rooted in waterfall methodologies, yet it is a much-needed leap to succeed when something entirely new is to be invented.

I would like to compare it to how one can plan for the unexpected. When the solution is still unknown, many will find it hard to say how much work it will take to create it. Either a huge additional amount is added for unknown risk, or one does not know how long it will take to get there. In place of having a detailed checklist for a valid use case, I believe it is sufficient to have a clear opinion about the ballpark of the development required.

It may also be useful to work in resources and timelines, not yet in currencies. This is because the varying number of zeros behind estimates may quickly change the tactics of how the solution should be developed. Should it happen locally, or should other solutions be sought? Some examples could be outsourcing development to another country, purchasing parts of the solution, or venturing into partnerships with parties that provide small or large parts of similar solutions. It all depends on the starting point and the desired outcome, yet there should be an idea of how much it will take to get the use case up and working.

You may be asking about the late appearance of this question: how much development would be required for a given use case? It is intentional that it appears at the last of the nine checkpoints validating use cases. The reason is partly that if this question comes earlier, there is a risk of spending more time and resources than needed contemplating the cost vs. value.

It is easy to get engulfed in the activity of bringing up estimates at an early stage. This in itself requires resources and slows down the process when deciding upon the validity of the use case. Endless discussions on financials have derailed entire use cases, let alone projects. This is why it is important to change the mindset of 'having to know' upfront to a belief-based statement of far more brevity that can be altered along the way. The shift from waterfall to agile is a huge cultural step for most organizations. To avoid the pitfall of spending any more time on financials in the early stages than necessary, the rough estimation of development required is therefore added as an early checkpoint when the use case is evaluated. More detailed planning may be required before scaling a use case, but until the case is proven, planning can be a waste of time.

As a guiding line, one may distinguish between backend and frontend development as a checkpoint. If one knows that major structural changes will be needed to succeed with the use case, it makes sense to articulate this as a large cost as early as possible. If the imagined UX is partly existing in a similar solution, one may downscale expected development in this part of the application accordingly. For example, one can use a percentage key to estimate what an average frontend for a comparable solution may cost. A sign of being too detailed at this stage is if you run out of space on your one-pager when estimating what needs to be developed.

HYPOTHESIS-DRIVEN INNOVATION

One of the greatest shifts in moving from traditional waterfall methodologies to agile methodologies is the mind shift. Increasingly often, it does not make sense to plan for everything ahead. Change tends to include cultural, organizational, and often personal dimensions. Agile is still seen by some as posing a threat to the established, planned, and structured way of creating new things. This skepticism is often due to a lack of knowledge and understanding about what agile is. I have seen many projects slowly become more successful as agile methodologies have been applied. Cultural, organizational, and personal focus is shifting from the control of great plans and even greater expenses towards increased focus on smaller chunks of deliverables. Frequent quality control of how each small part fits into a larger picture has increased in importance. Letting go of centralized control has made room for more realistic and dynamic control on a smaller scale.

The number of controlling mechanisms in older organizations has often been larger than in younger corporations. I have experienced internal control checkpoints for a single process requiring signatures outnumbering the number of employees in the entire company. That is to say, only the checks and controls necessary to get things done exceeded the capacity of the entire organization. This was before any core activity in projects or operations was performed at all. It is no wonder that the world has reacted by delegating checks and balances to be closer to where the action takes place and by increasingly making use of agile methodology.

By making shifts in the organization of where the gravitas of controls are performed, organizations have increasingly been freed from rigid top-down demands that have at times unduly added to the total burden of the organization. While management has spent time collecting large amounts of reports, domain experts and operators have spent time collecting vast amounts of detailed information for reporting. Agile thinking has eased the total amount of work due in many organizations. This is the consequence of applying overarching universal principles, looking towards the core of creativity and the lightest of processes possible without moving towards randomness.

What can innovation look like? The answer is strongly influenced by empirical methods. It may surprise some that it is mutually influenced by ancient practices of tribal decision-making that have existed universally around the planet for thousands of years. What I will refer to as hypothesis-driven use case development is not identical to either the empirical method or *Open Space Technology*. Inspiration and simplicity are drawn from both in a way that hopefully offers recognition to the many who are using agile and similar methods.

Looking at our nine dimensions regarding what makes any use case feasible, the availability of data ranks almost at the top, only surpassed by value. A clear problem statement definitely ranks close to or next to these two. I find the discussion as useful as the one about the chicken and the egg—you cannot have one without the other. For the sake of simplicity, I will start with the articulation of a clear problem statement in the area of use case application. This approach may seem a bit rigid, as we are in agile territory, and the culture of 'just starting to develop something' has been successful for many. The more rigid AS-IS analysis and TO-BE future ambitions are, the clearer it is that these are aging concepts in a number of organizations.

It is more and more rare that energy and time spent on mapping out where you are and where you are going pay off when the landscape keeps moving faster and faster. It makes sense to act more agile, to start walking, and to make directional adjustments along the way. Still, my belief is that it makes sense to apply the simplest layer of structure possible at any given time in the use case development process. This is a way of spending a minimum of effort to make sure that you always know, roughly or simply well enough, where you are and where the goal is. The hypothesis of the use case may change, or even collapse, along the way as the landscape keeps changing. Then it makes sense to know as soon as possible, so the approach and direction can be changed appropriately. Agile does not mean to walk and work blindly; it means to take smaller steps and then reorient as you go.

So, if the use case is formulated as a hypothesis, it makes sense to start with a clear problem statement that explains exactly what the problem is and exactly how it will be solved. In this scenario, your use case describes how it will be solved. You will need the problem statement as a basis to work on all the way from conception until you have the finished, scaled solution. Your problem statement needs to hit the mark throughout the lifetime of the solution. If the problem statement changes at any point in time, you may end up with an invalid use case. You should set yourself up to observe, understand, and gauge results in relation to your problem statement.

An example of a failed problem statement would be Kodak's. Their business model and hence human problem statement did not adjust when the global market for imaging went digital, resulting in the bankruptcy of the company. An example of a successful problem statement is Facebook. By successfully digitizing human relationships, they took over a substantial part of the world.

DATA LAYERS
Distinguishing between different types of data is a way to create structure in a world where endless numbers of opportunities can make choices harder to make. Structuring datasets by type, class, and nature can be an efficient way to carve out room for navigating opportunities. Understanding the nature of datasets and layering them in their natural order is useful when framing use cases. The actual sorting of data is not as important as the human mind grasping the undetected structures in the masses of data.

For any use case to be realized, relevant data needs to be available and accessible. When the availability of data is confirmed, the articulation of the actual problem and solution, as well as the use case, is clear. Then it makes sense to work a bit further with the structuring of the data. It makes sense to plan for how the data should be layered in the use case. Some use cases may have one set of data, while others may have many more. The more data available, the more opportunities there are for complex use

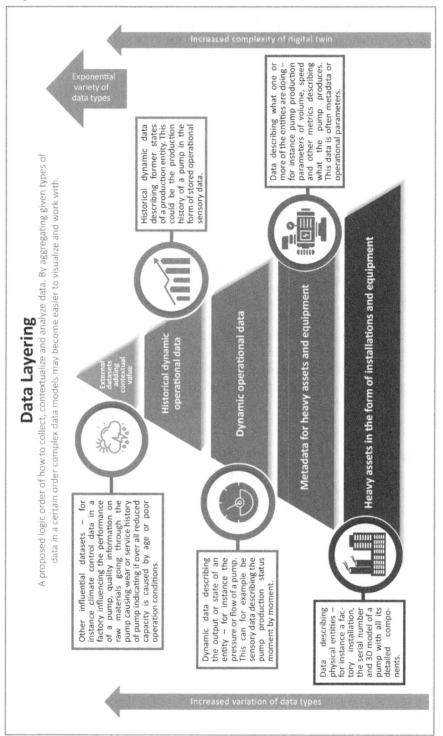

Diagram 2

Data Layering

A proposed logic order of how to collect, contextualize and analyze data. By aggregating given types of data in a certain order complex data models may become easier to visualize and work with.

Increased complexity of digital twin

Exponential variety of data types

Historical dynamic data describing former states of a production entity. This could be the production history of a pump in the form of stored operational sensory data.

Data describing what one or more of the entities are doing — for instance pump production parameters of volume, speed and other metrics describing what the pump produces. This data is often metadata or operational parameters.

External datasets adding contextual value

Historical dynamic operational data

Dynamic operational data

Metadata for heavy assets and equipment

Heavy assets in the form of installations and equipment

Other influential datasets — for instance climate control data in a factory influencing the performance of a pump, quality information on raw materials going through the pump causing wear or service history of pump indicating if over all reduced capacity is caused by age or poor operation conditions.

Dynamic data describing the output or state of an entity — for instance the pressure or flow of a pump. This can for example be sensory data describing the pump production status moment by moment.

Data describing physical entities — for instance a factory installation, the serial number and 3D model of a pump with all its detailed components.

Increased variation of data types

86

cases. **This is why it makes sense to start innovating digitally by looking at what data types are available inside and outside the organization, product, or service. The fidelity and quality of each dataset are important for the quality and success of digital innovation.**

In theory, there is no limit to how many layers of data may be applied in a use case. A mathematician may not set any limitations on how many variables there *could* be in an equation, but most definitely, the same mathematician could advise you on how many variables *should* be in an equation for you to still be capable of resolving it. Digitization of datasets has made it possible to include enormous amounts of variables in equations, but how many variables you may be comfortable working with within a parallel structure may be far less. In other words, the complexity of the use case is often dictated by the number of data layers included. After all, most digital use cases consist partly of digitized analytics or analytical models, so the complexity will vary widely depending on what the articulated problem and solution (use case) require.

A simple version of a use case is to throw a ball up into the air and then use the variables of time, speed, direction, and distance to analyze how fast and where the ball will hit the ground. A more complex variation of basically the same use case happened in April 1970, when NASA operations in Houston had to use the same variables of time, speed, direction, and distance to get Apollo 13 and its crew safely back home to Earth. The space version of the use case would be vastly more complex than the basic equation due to the additional variables and datasets required to find the solution.

For industrial use cases, it makes sense to layer datasets according to the complexity of the data itself. In some ways, it is like starting with one-dimensional constellations of data before adding two-dimensional and three-dimensional variables to the equation. This is an observation I have made when working with a number of use cases. In some cases, the order of datasets to be added may be done differently for any specific reason that applies to the unique context.

In most settings I have attended, there has been little or no attention paid to the order of data layering when starting out the search and collection of data. The attitude that any interesting data is good as a starting point is, of course, sensible. Yet this approach is wide, and in cases where a large number of datasets are available, it can be challenging to navigate an entire data scientist team through the selection process.

The multiple ways to understand the business value to be harvested from the data make the decision of what data to choose and focus on quite challenging. It can be a somewhat subjective and, at times, even random affair. Sure, a lot of use cases are developed for the purpose of learning, but in the end, the entire business may benefit from maximizing the learning over a given period of time. A conscious and structured approach to the layering of datasets may shorten the time it takes to create truly valuable use cases.

The idea to start with static, physical data is often a practical one. Get an overview of the equipment, hardware, physical product, or any sensibly sized physical entity on the table before starting to engage in the data information. Then check what the physical entity is actually *doing*. Consider this a basic map where the information needs to be detailed enough to be navigable but not so detailed that the reader gets overwhelmed and confused. What this level might be depends on the type of business, product, and organization combined. Just like project management methods deal with work breakdown structure, often called WBS, a similar way of thinking may be applied to how datasets are mapped. You should be able to get an overview from the map you create. Avoid fancy, attractive data analytics and be pragmatic so that you may find your data layering structure easier to work with and communicate to benefit others. (See diagram on page 86)

When a map, or choice, of basic dataset(s) are selected, it makes sense to choose another layer of data to contextualize the first data layer. Often, but not always, the second dataset will contain information about what the physical entities in the first dataset are *doing*. This could be metadata or variable properties of the first data layer. The first data layer may be many other things, but for the sake of simplicity in describing the principles of layering data, I will stick with metadata, for now, as metadata provides information about the entities described in the first data layer. This shows that the second data layer adds a layer of complexity and depth to the first data layer. It is as if we are adding some description and detail to the entities in our map. While the first dataset could represent physical production equipment, a typical second dataset could be the solution design or flow map for the same piece of equipment.

When two data layers are selected and described, it is often time to start adding dynamic data. This could be operational datasets or any set of information that can be measured and that changes over time. Now we can start to put some life into our map. We are adding temporary variables to our data analysis. This shift of focus often increases the possibilities of value creation from the use case exponentially. In a sense, we are moving into another dimension. We are not dealing with either static or dynamic data. By adding several, and differing, datasets into a layered context, we are quickly expanding the potential for the use case. Examples of such data could be any sensory data from meters, valves, speed, volume, pressure, temperature, sound, or a video feed related to the production equipment in some form.

A natural next step in adding another layer of data is to include historical data layers. This is a logical expansion of dynamic data layering. By adding historically layered data to the already temporary dynamic data, a new richness and depth to the map are forged. Historical datasets provide new opportunities for analysis that were not there before. Once more, we add complexity and expand the possibility of value creation in the use case exponentially. Examples are historical sensory data, ERP or legacy system data, supply chain history, or benchmarks of any kind.

After including historical data in our layers, the choices of datasets to be contextualized expand exponentially yet another time. Every new dataset adds an unaccounted number of opportunities. It starts to be a challenge to anticipate the quality of any next dataset to be included. The one shared trait would be that the next dataset to be represented in the layering will be different than any of the former data layers. For every dataset layered and contextualized, the number of opportunities for developing use cases goes fan-shaped, and the next dataset will be like a fork section in our map, leading to a high number of possible ways ahead. Often, such data sets are external to the original piece of metadata. Some examples of datasets added at this stage include a map layer, a 3D model of the production environment, weather data, personnel access management information, HSSQ routines, or any other external measurable factor that intrigues when contextualized with the formerly mentioned layers of data.

Most commercial use cases I worked on until 2010 stopped at the second last level of complexity. When the original source of data was not within the factory floor or enterprise, it was often referred to as a benchmark and incorporated in the data model in a less integrated manner. Often in the form of a checkpoint rather than a self-standing analytics solution. The internet opened up global software tools that included a large number of datasets. The value chain of each solution offered often ends at the end of the enterprise value chain. Not until the historical tipping point, when data was more generally seen as a commercial commodity, did full-blown solutions with value chains across fields, businesses, and seemingly unrelated datasets emerge on a large scale.

Process information can be applied to all layers. It is often introduced somewhere in the complexity level of dynamic and historical datasets, while all layers beyond static data can contain process information.

The maturation and shared understanding of data contextualization among commercial consumers have gradually opened the minds of business owners and domain experts alike. An increasing number of types and volumes of datasets are layered into an increasing number of use cases across most application areas. One example of this happening is the inclusion of Google Maps in numerous apps around the world. To mention some, there is a generic map added to traffic solutions, travel booking systems, utility solutions, flight surveillance solutions, transporting companies, and GPS trackers of any form and type.

Another example of how a sense of 'unlimited data' can be contextualized is the data layer of weather information. By adding weather data to personal navigation tools, an entirely new dimension of use has emerged. Not so many years ago, a GPS tracker was an invaluable device for any mountain guide. Today, any smartphone has GPS functionality embedded with a weather layer on top and a video function or slider showing the timeline for the weather in current and future time for any location selected. In the past, a mountain guide would check the weather forecast and keep track of the weather on the GPS device. I trust some still do so today. More recently, the possibility of seeing live weather reports as a dynamic data layer on top of the GPS data has provided value for many. This adds a selling point for personalized commercial GPS equipment compared to older units without this functionality.

I will attempt to make an analog comparison as an example to show how value can be added step by step over time. Take a coffee mug. Three thousand years ago, it would consist of a clay cup, and it was clear to all at the time what it was and what the value of it was. Then, at some point when hot beverages became popular, someone would add a handle to the cup, and that would make all the difference when the content was boiling hot. Perhaps a few centuries later, the invention of glazing would make the use of the cup more hygienic, easier to clean, more comfortable to the touch, and—not the least—more attractive to look at. More recently, a maker of cups would think of adding names to cups. Who would not like the sentimental value added by seeing his or her name on it and being able to distinguish it from other cups in a personal way? If you are into hiking, you may have seen collapsible and foldable cups in the outdoor store. So, the question is, what would you do with a cup if you could do absolutely anything to enhance it in any way you see fit? Being the digital nerd that I am, I would like to see the temperature of the contents of my thermal cup before letting my lips burn on hot coffee once more. This could, of course, be done in an analog way today, but for the sake of this example, I like the idea of turning a coffee cup into a digital product. And while I am at it, I would like the cup to remember my instinctual reaction of pulling the cup quickly away every time I still burn my lips because I forget to check the temperature before drinking my coffee. If the cup could remember over time what exact temperatures would create my abrupt reaction, it could over time build my personal benchmark temperature and perhaps even give me a red blinking light as a visual warning when the content of the cup is above this exact benchmark temperature. Then, because I get tired of a blinking light on my work desk, it should only blink when I pick it up. Remember, it already has a moving sensor built in. Then perhaps I would like this signal to be audio and not visual. And as the cup now already makes noise, perhaps it could wish me a good morning at 7:00 a.m. every morning too. I think this is a good moment to consider adding weather data and GPS location to the service the cup provides. And so it goes on. I know this chain of thought is a bit ludicrous, but it does express a process of how a product known to us all can turn digital and how functionality is added to most useful things over time, no matter if we discuss coffee cups or gas filters. After all, it is the value harvested from the insight or function added to a product compared with the investment required that often decides the crossroads where reality meets fantasy.

The general nature of the different complexity layers I have explained above is true for many use cases, but not all. The proposed structure of layering datasets according to static, dynamic, historic, and further unlimited qualities is based upon my involvement in developing various use cases. It is a way of approaching information analysis that has served me many times. Business management and domain experts must initially declare a common path to decide what data may prove to be the most valuable for the use case in question. One can also note that when vital datasets are missing in the process of selecting data, more often than not the root cause is found in poorly defined, or entirely lacking, problem statements. When one does not have a strong idea about what value the data will provide, it is difficult to choose the right types of data to innovate with in the first place.

I would encourage anyone framing use cases to play with and mix up the concepts of data layering. To some extent, it is a bit like playing with an equation where the problem is formulated as the question and the answer is formulated as the use case. Then it is a matter of search and match to find the variables belonging to the properties and values that constitute the datasets to be applied in the use case. Sometimes fewer datasets and fewer information layers are needed, while other times one can observe potential value by adding yet another nuanced data layer to the model.

I will move on to explain how one can approach data modeling in the first four data layers in an industrial context. There are no set rules as to how the type and order of data should be contextualized. I base my explanation on my experience of what has worked in industrial use cases when challenged by dataset contextualization. By layering heavy asset data, operational data, historical data, and unlimited data in the given order, I have created a meta-model of how information can be divided and layered in a workable way.

→ Heavy asset data
In the case of industrial data, it can make sense to start with production equipment. Often referred to as heavy assets. This is to start with an operable unit size defined as a unique entity. There may be one piece of equipment or several along a production line. It makes sense to start with an overview of which units are in scope for collecting data. It could be a constellation of various units or a collection of identical ones. An example of a data type is a serial number. The serial number makes the heavy unit both unique and traceable. In other cases, it may be sufficient to know the number of a specific type of asset along the production line. An example here would be knowing how many lighting units are required for an airport runway. Which light unit is placed exactly where might be less important than measuring the functionality of every light.

One may add another data layer consisting of the various parts each piece of equipment consists of. This can be useful, for instance, when the use case involves machine maintenance or production optimization for each unit. In other cases, it may not be necessary.

→ Operational data

When operational data is entered, complexity is added to the use case. We are moving from static to dynamic dimensions. Time stamps can be a central operational dataset, as can the pressure measurement of a valve during a given time span. And so the list goes on. The moment the dataset moves from a static to a dynamic nature, an exponential number of variables and datasets may be added, compared to the one-dimensional heavy equipment information. Variables within the dimensions of time, speed, pressure, weight, and volume can be dealt with, among so many others. Adding operational data as a concept after the first introduction of static equipment information opens up an enormous range of options for expanding use cases. While heavy asset information alone can be seen as a map, the addition of operational and temporal data may be seen as actual movement on the map. This additional dynamic layer makes the landscape so much more interesting and opens up more opportunities.

→ Historical data

When any type of information is captured and stored, we refer to it as historical data. Heavy asset data and operational data, as well as any other datasets, can be historical, given that information has changed at some point. The prerequisite is that the information be from the past. It makes sense to separate historical data from operational data in industrial use case development because not all operational data is recorded. This may be an unusual thought for millennials and younger, but it is still a reality in many operational facilities worldwide. By distinguishing between live operational and historical data, the data layering in a use case becomes easier to formulate.

→ Unlimited data

I have yet to encounter any limitations in applying layers to datasets. One can keep building layers of data around the initial heavy asset. In most cases, historically, the human mind has been the limiting factor in how data can be put to use. In the case of industrial facilities, it is now common to add layers of weather data, map data, financial data, and service management data, depending on what the use case demands. Immense amounts of data are opening up and becoming widely accessible worldwide. More external data may be applied to use cases than ever before. Market expansion, ocean climate monitoring, and galactic movements are only some of the areas being explored. There are so many others. Until recently, the human imagination has set the cap on opportunities for using datasets

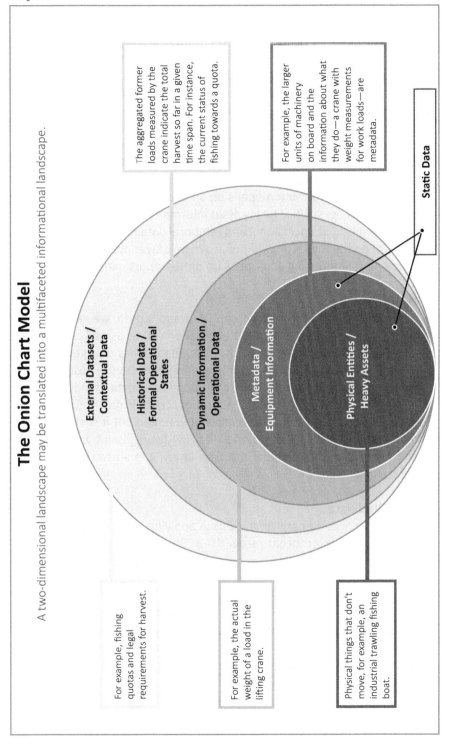

The Onion Chart Model

A two-dimensional landscape may be translated into a multifaceted informational landscape.

The aggregated former loads measured by the crane indicate the total harvest so far in a given time span. For instance, the current status of fishing towards a quota.

For example, the larger units of machinery on board and the information about what they do—a crane with weight measurements for work loads—are metadata.

Static Data

External Datasets / Contextual Data

Historical Data / Formal Operational States

Dynamic Information / Operational Data

Metadata / Equipment Information

Physical Entities / Heavy Assets

For example, fishing quotas and legal requirements for harvest.

For example, the actual weight of a load in the lifting crane.

Physical things that don't move, for example, an industrial trawling fishing boat.

Diagram 3

in structured ways. Now it is deep learning, and hence machines, that set limits on opportunities.

When I started working with data modeling, I had little experience with mathematics or equations. I didn't even know that what I did was data modeling. I had started out doing some basic computer programming and found the logic and simplistic structures of informatics alluring. I did have some experience in linguistics and the composition of metadata in linguistic grammar. I also had experience with music and the reading of sheet music for instruments, short scores, and orchestras. I could read music from one or several musical lines in parallel. In other words, I had a fair understanding of how language and music were constructed, also on an abstract meta-level.

By the time I started working with IT, I found that this basic understanding of how to apply structure to a theme was proving useful. Many will mistakenly look at language and music as two fields far apart. Yet if one explores the meta-level of informatics, mathematics, and physics, there are structures and exciting commonalities to be found.

At the beginning, when working with information datasets, I would place all my datasets along a line on a piece of paper. This was in the nineties, and I was trying my hand at programming. I would keep moving the different datasets back and forth along the line until I found a workable order and syntax in which to present a given data contextualization. Sometimes I would look up the code of different websites simply to learn how they were made. This was something I could present in a slide deck or explain on a timeline. At the time, this way of presenting data would be adequate to display the information needed when resolving a given problem statement.

A few years later, I came across what I refer to as an onion chart in my PowerPoint. Microsoft calls this a "stacked friend diagram." I could see an increasing number of peers using the onion chart to represent overlapping relationships, or what I call the contextualization of information. The onion graphically shows how datasets can be layered and how one dataset, or one piece of information, can be added to another to create a two-dimensional landscape of information in the form of a stack. This was, in some ways, not much more complex than my linear presentations back in the nineties, but I did find that the onion chart model made it easier for me to communicate to others how I intended to work with datasets. The enhanced visual presentation made it easier to challenge peers to add yet another layer to the onion instead of referring to the end of a linear chain of arguments.

By 2012, my mind had graduated to observing data constellations as a Rubik's Cube™. I suspect this was a consequence of repeatedly observing more complex use cases utilizing datasets in commercial tech solutions. My maturity and understanding of data contextualization was following the evolving mainstream perception of technology in the current markets I was operating in. I realized I needed to rise to the challenge of not only visualizing general models in 3D but also to visually contextualize datasets in 3D to grasp more complex data modeling. After all, I was working in a rather abstract realm, and I had to find ways to present my abstract ideas to consulting clients and peers alike. The idea of 3D matured for me when I was challenged by a bookkeeping task where I had to present a given number of accounting values in a prioritized and weighted way. I ended up applying a 3D model of data representation where moving one parameter or value around resulted in all others falling down in different places. In my mind, I was playing a game of 3D Tetris.

Within a couple of years, my mental Rubik's Cube™ was evolving rapidly. I needed more shapes beyond a cube to portray the imagined contextualization of data. A natural next step from the cube was the five-sided pyramid, then a sphere or tube. The physical shapes representing data models were becoming increasingly complex.

My understanding deepened, and I became fascinated by crystals and the process of crystallization of materials. To me, the process of crystallization represented how matter, or in other words, data, can hold a liquid form and then, by introducing a set of given conditions, crystallization will start from a single point and move outward, touching other points that crystallize under identical conditions. Within a time span given by known conditions, a block of solid crystal will be formed. To me, this process is a symbol of change and a natural example of how certain conditions change datasets into structures. The way fluidity transforms into recognizable forms and vice versa by the reversed melting process reminds me that there is no limit to what the contextualization of datasets may look like. In the same way, there is no limit to the variations of crystal structures. The bigger the structure, the more unique it is and the more possibilities it contains.

This is how I think about data modeling today, like having the opportunity to form a huge crystal to my own liking. My imagination sets the limit on complexity and the number of layers. I consider my perceived reality to be the greatest obstacle. I believe it is possible to express anything a human can observe or imagine in a data model, while datasets form the language of each unique model. Beyond the limitations of the human mind, deep learning evolves.

FUNCTIONALITY OFFERED

When data layers are recognized and pronounced in the enterprise landscape, it is time to focus on what specific functionality the use case in question will offer. This is to formulate a logical consequence for the solution offered to the problem. The data layering needs to support what the solution will actually do or deliver so that the functionality offered is clearly reflected in the solution to the problem statement. This is done by defining exactly and briefly what functionality will be provided. This is to define what the solution to the problem statement will actually *do*.

There is no use digging out data if it is not clear what the data modeling will provide. If the hands-on functionality offered by the use case is not well defined, it will be challenging to pinpoint exactly what the effect and value creation of the use case will be. The functionality offered by the use case should be more detailed than the effect of the use case, and it may describe the *how* of the use case. The functionality offered should be an operational description of how the solution or product will practically manifest. No matter if the functionality is a new dataset providing insight, a tangible product, a service, a market accelerator, or anything else, it needs to be detailed so that the solution will be easier to build. There also needs to be a tangible connection between the idea and the final value creation of the use case.

If it is unclear among the involved parties what the functionality of the use case actually is, it makes sense to play around with different articulations of what the use case will actually *do* as well as what the use case will directly *provide*. When the actual use case and the proposed value creation are both on the table, it will be easier to see what functionality supports both ends of the hypothesis: the *how* and the *value*.

Keep in mind that the model is dynamic and logical, so when changes are made, there will be ripple effects trickling down the entire model. If the imagined functionality of the use case changes, it could influence the effect and the real value creation of the use case. This should be kept in

Diagram 4

Hypothesis Driven Use Case

Describing the sequence of how specific, tangible value is created

Data Layers:
- Data describing physical entities (e.g., a storage facility—building and area information stored electronically)
- Metadata describing equipment parameters (e.g., operational metrics like climate control are parameters used by a digital system solution)
- Dynamic operational data (e.g., temperature measurements, data collected with sensors)
- Historical operational data (e.g., information on how many people have been in the building the last week and temperature fluctuations in various parts of the building) is stored in a database or in the cloud
- Other influential datasets (e.g., status information on physical entities provided by an alarm system—door and roller door status collected with sensor technology)

Functionality offered:
- Use case description (e.g., by using a Microsoft Azure dashboard, it is possible to combine the above-mentioned datasets and apply analytics with the goal of maximizing heat retention in a building during the winter)
- Benefits of the use case:
  - By observing repeated rapid and long-lasting temperature falls at specific locations in the building, one can also look at how the status of doors and roller doors from the alarm system together can provide power-consuming hot spots in the building mass.
  - By applying stricter status control and automatic actions to physical power-consuming hot spots in the building, less power may be consumed for heating.

Effects:
- Convert benefits to measurable effects:
  - Measureable financial value (e.g., a reduced power bill measured in USD)
  - Measurable HSSQ effects (e.g., employees experience an improved work climate inside; this can be measured with Questback tools)
  - Production optimization (e.g., improving the operational cost management of building mass)
- Visibility (e.g., the reputation of being a climate-friendly storage space provider in the market through applying continuous improvement to internal operations)

Hypothesis on value creation:
- Tangible, measurable KPIs that can be quantified and scaled according to the learning experience.
  - Financial value (e.g., KPI of reducing power consumption by 5% over a four-month winter period)
  - HSSQ (e.g., employees ratings of the work environment improve by 10%)
  - Production optimization (e.g., KPI to become ISO compliant with the required ISO standard, for instance ISO 9000 or ISO 45001)
- If the direction of the KPI deviates in addition to scaling, turn to the "fail fast" approach.
  - E.g., employees don't mind the cooler work environment enough to justify the cost of installing more sensors in power-consuming hot spots.
  - E.g., power-consuming hot spots in the building mass may overlap with access security high-risk areas as reported by the security division. The aggregated value of the original power consumption use case with a use case related to building access security qualifies for replication of the use case at other storage facilities.

mind at any time when one offer of functionality is overtaken by another, perhaps more alluring, based on the feasibility of the data layers offered. It can be tempting for many leaders to change the direction of the use case when the possibilities of functionality and capabilities of data mining are unraveled. In fact, agile methodologies encourage changes of direction when opportunities are observed. Still, it makes sense to complete the logic of the hypothesis-driven use case development. This is because the model provides a map between the original problem statement and the target of the desired value creation.

The map will likely provide many different options on how to get from a problem statement to tangible value creation. But if the road varies significantly from the original destination of value creation, there will be a need for another map. To put it bluntly, if you travel overland from Paris to Berlin, you may consider changing maps if you decide to make a detour via Moscow. You need to decide which road to take between the two cities, as venturing partway on various roads will only postpone your final arrival. Good ideas erupting along the way to a defined destination may make for a great journey, but they can also hamper, dilute, or even completely miss out on the desired result.

EFFECT

Most current models I have observed for use case and business development include the dimension of effect in some form to measure the validity of the use case. My challenge when working with only effect without venturing on to more detailed definitions of value creation is that effect is often too vaguely defined to evaluate at an early stage. I have seen effects such as convenience and efficiency implemented in many use cases where no tangible parameters have been aimed for. While many find it satisfying to define a general area of effect before moving ahead with a use case, I would recommend challenging the imagination to venture further until tangible detail is on the table. Before we can get to the point of tangible value creation, it is necessary to clearly map out one or more areas where the use case is expected to have the greatest effect.

Before any tangible value may be imagined as a result of any use case, the area of effect needs to be defined. In the same way, I imagine structured data layers form the grammar and language of a use case, and the functionality offered will be a tangible product or service. The effect will form the highest level of currency from which the value of the use case will emerge.

Later, I will go further into depth on how to work with the breakdown of values in use cases. For now, I will propose to work with the following high-level areas of effect:

- Execution efficiency
- Process improvement
- Product improvement
- Health and safety
- Visibility

In my years working with industrial use cases, I have not yet come across a use case that did not fit into one of these five categories. This is why I recommend using these five areas of effect to gauge the area of expected benefit for each use case.

→ Execution efficiency

Here I point towards any effect in the form of operational efficiency. An example to explain what efficiency is in this context can be made using a Texan oil pump transporting oil from an underground reservoir to an oil tank on ground level. These are often referred to as nodding donkeys. The efficiency is simply the output of the pumping action. There are strictly speaking only two ways to increase the execution efficiency of a pump: you can increase the volume of the oil pipe connected to the pump, or you can increase the speed at which the pump operates. In other words, the only two parameters that really matter are volume and speed.

→ Process improvement

This area of effect is a result of *how* the execution of a given operation is performed. Process improvement has been a popular task for various fields of consultants for years, and the LEAN framework has been some sort of holy grail for several decades when it comes to how to improve operational effects in the industrial world. By performing a task in a faster, cheaper, or somehow better way than before, money and time are saved. Process improvement is a way to do a task in a more efficient way than before.

→ Product improvement

When a use case improves the product, either by altering it or improving its quality, the result is distinguishable from the other four areas mentioned here. I mentioned the nodding donkey when I explained execution efficiency above. When the nodding donkey cannot improve the quality of the oil itself, it makes sense to isolate the effect of the use case. Changes to the core product may then be measured separately. A cost-versus benefit analysis is often required to determine if the investment will be worthwhile for the product to be altered.

→ Health and safety

Health and safety impose hugely differing priorities, applications and forms across various industries worldwide. Nevertheless, in the industrial field, it has surprised me how often use cases aimed to impact execution efficiency and process improvement in particular, have become stellar use cases for health and safety.

One example is the process improvement of using robots along almost any production line in the world. The intentional use case has more often than not initially been to secure a more accurate and precise execution of a process, as well as optimize the execution of the operational task at hand. By achieving increased control of the operational environment through the use of robots, one has simultaneously increased the safety of the workers on the production floor. When every move and execution of a programmed robot is predictable to the millimeter and millisecond, there is also a significantly reduced risk of unexpected injury to any personnel on the floor. When floor personnel are removed to external control rooms, the health and safety conditions of the production environment improve exponentially for the involved domain operators.

→ Visibility

In some cases, the mere need for visibility can be impactful enough to justify the complete development and scaling of a use case. One example would be any industry with a deep-rooted image of non-compliance in some form. An obvious example of a highly valuable use case would be to observe how the diamond mining industry has introduced a quality certification of how every diamond is produced according to predefined ethical standards. *The Kimberley Process Certification Scheme* is an example of how information regarding the origin of diamonds has been tracked to ensure the precious stones have been extracted without conflict. The efficiency of this certification scheme has been questioned by several organizations during the last decade. Still, it is an example of how certain details about the origin of a product can be tracked.

Another example is how the fruit industry intermittently applies similar supply chain tracking so that the supermarket customer can observe, by using an app or going online, exactly which farm, village, and country a specific piece of fruit is originating from. One may argue that such use cases add value to the product itself in the form of marketing content. One can also observe that the visibility of the use cases is valuable in itself. Value could, for instance, be aimed at compliance, branding value, or expanding market share. Still, the initial intended effect is directed towards increasing their visibility globally. After defining visibility as the core effect of the use case, there may be a more detailed division of effects working towards specific value creation. It can make sense to go with the affected area of visibility, as the more detailed nuances mentioned already move towards complexity and complicity.

THE HYPOTHESIS OF VALUE CREATION

Now we are approaching the golden nugget of hypothesis-driven use case development. As already mentioned, most overarching frameworks I have come across when developing use cases have stopped short of naming tangible and definite values. The reason for stopping short of naming the expected effects of the use case and not including the tangible value creation is often that when innovating, the entire landscape is new and one cannot know exactly what to expect. In other words, leadership and domain expertise prefer not to *commit* to the expected value creation of an imagined use case before it is proven. I will mildly suggest that this often originates in an enterprise-wide culture of not taking personal risks, or it may simply be an HR issue of not clearly linking results to roles throughout the organization. In either case, I do believe many companies are losing time and wasting efforts when a clear hypothesis of value creation is not driving the development of use cases efficiently.

There needs to be a balance between commitment and frequently gauging the hypothesis with the belonging stages. There needs to be flexibility and agility available to make the changes and analyze the hypothesis as soon as they are required. It demands a fine balance. The alternative when working with almost any innovative use case development is costly, at best. At worst, it is fully possible to develop malfunctioning use cases that are tied to individual prestige and ambition in the organization. These are use cases that seldom provide the value expected in the first place.

The hypothesis of value creation should stay current at every stage of development and level of leadership. The development should be closely monitored during the different stages of development to make sure that the potential value is valid at any given moment in the lifetime of the use case.

The hypothesis of value creation should always be tangible. It can be useful to connect it to a measurable strategy for the deliverables of the organization or enterprise as a whole. The following are examples of what such tangible values could look like:

- Improved execution efficiency in the nodding donkey results in 5% improvement in oil flow to the surface.
- Decreased production time per batch of freshly baked goods frees up the production floor so that 1,000 more loaves are produced daily.
- The increased quality of the composite material of sneaker products results in a 3% increase in market share.
- The introduction of robots on the production floor reduces the need for man-hours present on the floor from 45,000 hours per year to 1800 and reduces the risk of any personal injury by 95%.
- Improved visibility of the product supply chain for bananas results in improved trust in the brand, driving a 2% increase in market share.

VALUE STREAM BREAK DOWN AS A NAVIGATION TOOL

Every business and industry is unique, and attachment to what constitutes value creation varies widely from company to company. Much of the world is working exclusively with financial currencies when dealing with value creation. This does not mean that other currencies to measure value don't exist, as other areas of effect can create different kinds of value.

Using other forms of measuring value other than financial currencies is often avoided. This is because it is perceived as challenging to work in a uniform way with various types of value creation. Some examples of units that can be translated into financial currency are hours spent, tons of steel (or quantities of other resources) used, cubic meters of bunker oil spent, or kilowatts per hour. These are all tangible measures, but they are difficult to compare to each other. Hence the universal solution and culture of counting money. Work hours are converted to aggregated cost per resource; tons of steel are converted to the cost of steel; cubic meters of bunker oil are converted to fuel costs; and kilowatts per hour are converted to heating costs. This is how the world operates much of the time for the sake of simplicity, yet it should not prove too difficult to think differently and work with various currency units for measuring effect if we only choose our currencies wisely.

The UN sustainability goals set up in 2015 are an example of how new and relevant areas of effect, and hence currencies, can be defined. A number

Diagram 5

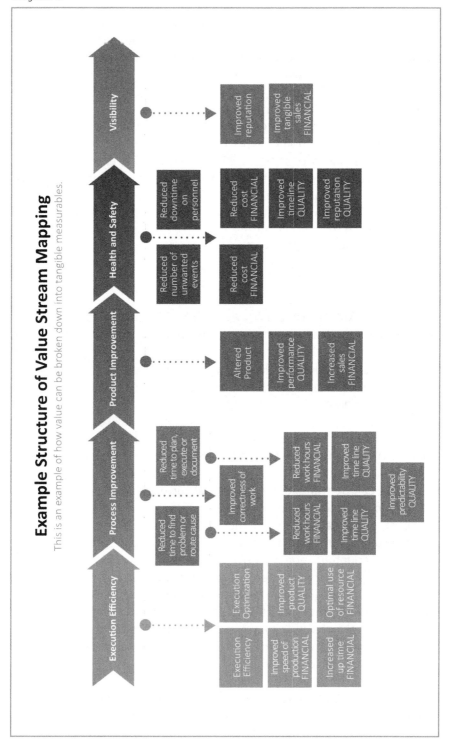

Example Structure of Value Stream Mapping

This is an example of how value can be broken down into tangible measurables.

of approaches as to how the 17 different areas of effect can be measured are underway or already established.

Historically, almost any commercial effect has been measured in a monetary currency in some way and at some point. The more commonly used areas of effect that are not financial are those of quality and HSSQ. In the end, these two areas are often measured in monetary terms.

For the sake of simplicity and to provide a clear example of value chain breakdown in this book, the most detailed conceivable effects described in this chapter are finance and quality. Keep in mind that the breakdown I present is merely an example that can be interchanged with the properties and structural approach according to each unique use case. The way I portray the breakdown of the value chain here has worked well for me in many use cases, while others may find that different structures and nominators work better for them. The principle of value chain breakdown is more important than any rule to be found in detail and content.

To work efficiently with tangible values in industrial environments, it makes sense to define the value in one or more of the following five areas of value creation:

- Execution efficiency
- Process improvement
- Product improvement
- Health and safety
- Visibility

On page 104, a diagram shows an overview of how a value chain breakdown can be done. In short, it is based on how to bridge the five areas of effect already mapped out, aiming to deliver tangible value in quantitative and qualitative parameters:

I believe that many organizations live in a culture where commitment to such tangible values is either too strict and narrow or too vague and not well defined. Keeping close track of a value breakdown structure following the Value Stream Mapping model in parallel with the stages of hypothesis-driven use case development is vital. It is possible to apply the lightest of structures needed to keep an eye on the day-to-day status and viability of the use case. When the landscape changes, it is relatively easy and fast to change the map accordingly.

I once heard of a car manufacturer that committed to producing 30% more cars during the following calendar year by introducing use cases involving machine learning to eradicate bottlenecks in the production line. This in itself is a brilliant idea that is becoming more feasible to achieve by the month in the current automation market. Unfortunately, plans and details on how to achieve this ambitious goal of a 30% improved production rate were lacking, leaving the commitment unrealistic. It is common for top management to set clear KPIs of this kind and then allow the organization to follow them as best they can to achieve such goals. This can work very well when execution, process, product, HSSQ, and visibility are rigged for success. But if transparency and overview of such value chains are weak, such a push may soon end up backfiring. The act of closely monitoring all stages of hypothesis-driven use case development together with the expected value creation breakdown structure places the right balance of control and agility on the development process.

Some may find it useful to match and mix between different areas of effect and different currencies of value in their own unique value breakdown structure. Some may work the model bottom-up and others in the top-down direction. Others may not know where to start and end up starting with a single known point in the very middle because this is the only recognizable point in their organization. Then they work their way outwards in the model, mapping their way as they go in a more random direction. However, the exact model used is not paramount; the principle of applying structure is more important.

In this part, we have explored *how* digital transformation and the development of use cases can be controlled by applying the lightest amount of structure. The nine dimensions of navigation are needed to keep the developing path in sight at all times, from beginning to end. Hopefully, this will show everyone involved in digital transformation a way through necessary change that leaves them with the opportunity to navigate digital transformation with confidence. By following the given path of principles, value creation is at the center of any digital endeavor.

In the fourth and last part of this book, we venture further into the current landscape of digital transformation and look at how boundaries are not only being pushed open faster than ever before but also how disruption is happening all around us today. We are all part of this evolutionary spectacle, willingly or not, so we can choose to take part in it proactively instead of merely reacting.

The visions at play today are intimidating at best and devastating at worst. Yet the way disruption plays out globally, we can turn the confusion stage into preparation and actionable steps to manage and set a clear pathway through encompassing change. To make technology work for us and not against us, we first need to understand what it is all about and recognize the quantum levels of change from a human perspective, which is beyond what many of us do today.

The fourth part of this book builds on the understanding of the first three parts. It will portray some real and some potential ways ahead for digital transformation and what it can provide in the time to come. It challenges our minds to anticipate the continuation of where we are and encourages us to observe the larger patterns of how digitalization transforms our world. If we can learn to better see the changes as they happen, I believe that will empower us to apply ourselves better to the pace of development happening today.

PART 4

NAVIGATING TECH DISRUPTION

A GENERAL MATURITY MODEL ON INNOVATION

For use case development to be successful, a few parameters in the checklist of nine points are absolutely required to be present for successful innovation to take place. For many years, I believed, wrongfully, that organizations that had sufficient funding for innovation would be relatively successful at it. It turned out I was not only wrong, but with time I could observe a lot of successful innovations emerge from organizations with severe limits on available funding. The lack of resources and falling behind in the market have forced many companies to find new solutions to known problems in addition to adjusting to the way operations are done. Companies with limited funding often have to change their approach entirely to save money, work more efficiently, and create bigger margins in their business.

One example of how scarcity has propelled innovation to success is the water scarcity in the agricultural industry. By applying machine learning to how and when water is distributed across larger crops to maximize yield, the agricultural industry is an example of how the scarcity of a resource has driven technological advancements.

Another example is the segment of road transport that generally works within the strict economic confines of small margins due to strong competition and a high number of players in the market. The small margins of the business have contributed to the recent reduction of operational costs. An entire shift in the traditional domain of transport towards new emerging business models of mobility has changed the competitive landscape of transport in recent years. Where buses, bicycles, and private cars used to be seen as some sort of competitors in the cityscape, the emergence of driverless buses, bike lanes, and carpooling models are changing the lives of both bus drivers and car owners. Bus drivers can expect a decrease in demand for their services, while city dwellers may not need to cash out for an expensive personal parking space as the carpooling model may cover the need. In recent years, the shift has moved towards a more holistic view of mobility, where new options and business models are introduced.

Citizens may perceive this shift as a way to have cheaper and smoother movement in their daily lives. In parallel, the bus driver may perceive the most significant disruption as his or her job is eliminated. The increased focus on reducing the cost of mobility services is removing human roles from the operations. Arguments for reduction of CO_2 emissions, ease of movement, and accurate human transport across cities are emphasized. I believe the cost parameter is the driving force in the change of transport business models towards currently emerging mobility principles, while often climate effects are fronting the changes commercially. Without the cost savings in the emerging business models, fewer stakeholders and decision-makers would find them valid.

At the other end of the corporate scale of wealth, I imagined the oil and gas industry and those operating companies to be overflowing with funding for innovation. Again, I was mistaken, as it has taken this industry a long time to modernize, change, and innovate compared to similar industries. One example is the aviation industry, which has been decades ahead in the introduction of fairly basic digital use cases, providing huge benefits. It was the need for operational robustness that drove the aviation industry to adopt the global use of serial numbers for the sake of tracing aircraft and their components. The importance of insight into the history and status of each specific part of an aircraft drove the introduction of unique serial numbers for each component in aircraft carriers.

It was not a lack of funding that made the oil and gas industry a conservative actor on the stage of innovation. The oil and gas industry was slower to introduce and adapt to the global application of serial numbers, as well as similar digital use cases, because a fast innovation pace had not been a deciding factor for success in the market. Highly profitable, well-established companies are often not dependent on innovation for survival. This is true only to the point where the market is disrupted by new technology or products.

Few cases are better known than when the current leading global producer of photographic analog film underestimated the disruption of digital photography. I have already mentioned Kodak, which ended up being an outdated global company within a few years between the 1990s and 2012, when the company filed for Chapter 11 bankruptcy protection in the USA. By the time the failed call of judgment from top management dawned, it was too late to change the direction of the company.

When looking at the nine checkpoints for evaluating use cases, the three first ones stand out as exhaustively necessary for a use case to succeed. There has to be at least one problem (or opportunity for benefit) present that the use case will resolve. There needs to be data or information available to resolve the problem or contribute to a benefit being realized. Finally, there needs to be some promise of value, at least at some stage in the life cycle of the use case. *Problem, data, and value* are absolute requirements for a use case to be successful.

The following six checkpoints described in "Part 3" of this book can be showstoppers if not sufficiently in place and mitigated, yet they are also negotiable. Between problem, data, and value, the first and the last are usually by far the easiest to nail down. Everyone has problems, and wherever a problem can be solved, there is value to be found. If not, there was likely no problem in the first place. Finding data in the form of information turns out to be by far the most practically challenging of the three.

Today, data is everywhere. Yet much of it is just noise due to a lack of quality and structure. Available data is often hard to extract. It may be polluted, inconsistent, incomplete, or contained in a less than ideal format. In my experience, the majority of time and resources spent on use case development are spent searching for and making the right data available.

The common approach of looking for data before starting to look for use cases is a pragmatic way to approach use case development, and it works for many. However, I lean towards starting with the business problem as an opportunity to maximize the output value of any use case. This should not be left to coincidence but rather be weighed against the available data. Some may be less concerned whether the task starts with a problem statement or with looking for data, yet I insist on following the leading beacon of business value when working with use cases. To me, this is a question about being either more forward-leaning about creating business value or opting to let the data drive the direction of the use case. In the end, both dimensions need to be monitored closely, while I prefer the search and mining of data to be business-driven.

It should be mentioned that there is a fairly recent best practice available for innovation: the ISO56000/2020 on innovation management. It describes the vocabulary, fundamental concepts, and principles of innovation management and its systematic implementation. Personally, I think this standard is a good start, particularly in defining a shared vocabulary when innovating. At the same time, I don't find it detailed enough yet to avoid the hindrances that almost any innovation project would encounter. I do understand that ISO standards are general and intend to show the way for many, and in this way they are applicable to many. Perhaps I should not expect it to be much more detailed, as it would then also be more limited in the area of its application. This conundrum of general vs. detailed approaches is something I discuss in several parts of this book. It is hard to agree on a sweet spot between the two. To me, the ISO56000/2020 forms a good theoretical model, and I hope it will evolve further in the years to come and bring even more value to its users. The upcoming ISO/AWI/56000 is under development, and I am sincerely looking forward to holding it in my hands. Until then, I find "Part 3" of this book a pragmatic attempt to navigate digitized innovation and product management that will not conflict in any way with the ISO56000/2020 but rather complement it by adding dimensions, nuance, and detail.

SHARED TRAITS OF WELL-PREPARED ORGANIZATIONS
There are definitely business areas and organizations that are better pre-pared for harvesting value from data than others. Highly digitized orga-nizations and businesses are generally better prepared to succeed with innovative digital use case development than others that are less rich in the digital realm. This digital maturity comes down to culture, traditions, margins in the market that allow for the status quo to continue, conserva-tive or progressive leadership, and so many other factors. Still, one of the most important factors is the *availability of good data*. Among industrial use cases, there are some levels of maturity that can be recognized. In the past, enterprises have often built and selected a data strategy in the best

of times. In the worst of times, there have been no strategies or conscious approaches to data. When leadership has kept the focus on business goals, the understanding of approaching data consciously has not always been present.

Many IT directors have been delegated the task of sorting out a plan for company-wide handling of master data in a way that makes them feel a bit alone and detached from the core business of the company. IT has been considered a necessary cost by many top managers, so data has not been considered the source of business opportunities as it should have been. Planning and handling of master data have often been delegated to middle managers who have had little mandate to act proactively or do much more than keep track of data in a reactive manner. Over the last decade, more and more companies have adopted a new mindset when it comes to data. Instead of thinking of IT as merely tools to make their production and business work, more are looking at digitalization as a way to operate and steer the enterprise more efficiently and accurately.

Today, many companies consciously build their organizations and operations digitally before the analog version is realized. By utilizing master data as an internal driver for any change process, companies are now optimizing their business and operations worldwide. This reflects a forward-leaning way to use data and a progressive attitude towards IT. It can also be a cheap, accurate, and controlled approach to building internal and external infrastructure. By modeling any company and production data digitally, decisions on scaling, timelines, and change processes can be assessed before they are put into motion.

Digitalization has been a prerequisite for global outsourcing and insourcing of operations over the last few decades. When services and production facilities are gradually moved to third and fourth countries or returned to their original production country, the digitalization required to support remote functions opens up a lot of opportunities for yet more digital use cases. Companies that have kept changes to a minimum and not consciously used data-driven models for core business tasks are less prepared for further application of digital use cases than companies that have been consciously collecting datasets for years.

Imagine a local fishing boat off the northern coast of Norway. For decades, digital navigation tools and marine echo-sounder tech have been standard equipment on board any fishing vessel. Yet it has taken a long time to collect the data from these tools and apply the historic datasets to digital use cases. The experience, and hence domain expertise, has been kept in the heads of the fishermen themselves and the knowledge of where the fish are to be found has not been an easily shared secret, at least not to outsiders. The introduction of digital use cases extending the product line of marine echo-sound equipment to offer analytics of where and when the biggest and highest number of fish may be found over time has taken a long time to reach the market. Marine scientists may own much of the existing data of this type today and could, obviously, be more interested in developing use cases for conservation purposes. The tech competence threshold among local fishermen may be a bottleneck for the application of advanced digital use cases in the industry, yet I suspect that the cultural setting of working with analog methods is deeply ingrained in the domain culture.

In 2001, when the Swedish oil and gas exploration and production company Lundin Energy was formed, the company had a strong focus on building the enterprise digitally as well as physically. The result is a modern, forward-leaning company that can drive both business and internal changes based on data modeling. Having good digital control and high-quality sets of master data company-wide has become a competitive edge. Both digital control and quality data open up opportunities for accurate decision-making, nuanced historic business analysis, and wide-ranging business and operational prediction models, among other things. The opportunities for value creation stemming from what starts to look like a digital enterprise model are many and big. Many companies wish they were where Lundin is. A late start to digitizing internal organizations and operations has led to many organizations falling behind when it comes to the successful application of digital use cases.

There is some irony in the fact that it takes an open, digitally conscious culture, some street smarts, and often less advanced digitalization to get going with valuable digital use cases. To have a fully digitized twin of an enterprise is not a goal in itself. The goal is to have the important datasets, to have high-quality and accessible data, and to understand how to develop the most valuable digital use cases with the resources available in the first place. It is not the number of datasets available that determines the value of each use case; it is the business value available from the use of datasets that is at the core of digital use case development success.

DATA LAYERING AND DIGITALIZATION MATURITY

In the chapter referring to data layering, I have mapped out a suggestion for how the contextualization of datasets may be dealt with in a structured way. This approach is far from set in stone. It is a huge step towards digital maturity for any company to understand which datasets are important to their unique value streams, organization, products, and business. It makes sense to start collecting data on tangible, measurable units and then to keep expanding the digitization towards more complex and peripheral data collections. *Both the level of complexity of the data collected and the shared understanding of how available data can be layered and contextualized directly reflect the digital maturity of the enterprise or company.* It reflects on the digital preparedness and agility of the organization through each of the nine use case readiness checkpoints listed in this book.

It is surprising to see how conservative, static mastodon companies, including some of the largest global corporations, are portraying themselves as cutting-edge technology drivers in the market. Indeed, image is everything. All it takes is a look under the hood to see how digitally adept and agile some of these companies really are. A bit of analysis of recently published digital use cases can be revealing. The task of looking at the actual wiring of digital use cases can be a challenge for anyone on the outside. To know how a corporation really deals with the digital present and future, examine the variety and nature of data collection, the complexity of data layering, and contextualization, then put it all together. Particularly in the area of corporations and operations.

From the outside, one can also, with some skill, observe some aspects of the general cultural perception of digitalization across the enterprise. Corporate and employee social media presence, or the lack of it, can be revealing. If it turns out that the corporation relies heavily on external partners for technology development, one may ask what the core business of the corporation really is. If the answer is analog, then it is likely that the corporation will be culturally analog and less focused on master data. There can be a given path to get to the most valuable digital use cases in the shortest amount of time. Starting with a digital representation of a given, smaller area and then fleshing out the digitized landscape until more processes are reached (or disruptively eliminated). Then the core production value stream follows. Finally, the product itself is influenced by concerted digitalization efforts company wide.

It is fully possible to start anywhere on this path. Many start digitizing the product at once. It depends on unique circumstances whether an organization is ready to move straight to the digital use case relating to the core product or not.

It is a timely observation that the divide in the world as we know it will keep increasing between those who have a little and those who have a lot. Just like the divide between landowners and tenants has existed for thousands of years and has continued in society, dividing the rich and the poor, we are now in the information age, where a new divide between those who have a wealth of data and the 'have-nots' is growing.

We are still at a stage in our information revolution where there is a lot of fascination with hardware and what can be done with it. Slowly, more people are realizing that hardware is fantastic, but without data to run on it or new information resulting from the application of hardware, hardware in itself is not worth much in the digital transformation.

Not long ago, I was faced with industry domain experts who were super excited about newly purchased robots for inspection purposes at operational production plants. I intentionally tried not to reduce their excitement about their purchase. Something I silently, and perhaps arrogantly, regarded emotionally as similar to buying a new toy. I can only hope that I encouraged their excitement about what the robot could provide in terms of digital use cases. The information an inspection robot can collect is the most exciting part to me, far more so than the fact that it can actually perform inspections. The dataset collected with sensor technology is what provides the value, not the capacity of the inspection itself. It is a bit like buying a new car with lots of new technological features. It looks beautiful, and it is a fascinating creation, but for the majority of people, it will mostly provide value by driving. Some additional value will come from embedded technology, like the navigation system, climate control, and four-wheel traction control.

One of the first times I came home with a new PC, I was so happy to show it around to my family members. I found the mouse pad intriguing; it's Bluetooth as well. I liked the benefits they gave me for both work and play. It was a real challenge to impress my grandmother, though. She had lived her entire life in analog and could not possibly see the same value as I did in this flashy new plastic container (PC). She had heard about people paying their bills 'online' but could not see the benefit over going directly to the bank. It was a challenge for me to communicate the digital benefits when she did not perceive them as a value in her worldview. She was always happy living her highly analog life, and I cannot imagine her choosing differently if she were given the option. There are days I envy her calm, slow-paced life and vantage point. At the same time, I would not like to miss the digital opportunities of realizing potential, ideas, and inventions or being creative in the same realm as my peers in time and society. To be able to extract high value from any invention, it is necessary to speak the language of the time when the invention existed. To understand the context in which the invention will function, insight into how to use digital tools is essential.

Try to imagine a week without a smartphone. There are people who do it, but they are also paying the price of not being involved in the actions around them compared to their peers. A few still choose a non-digital life and are happier for it. Others cannot go digital for educational reasons. No matter what the reason is, choosing not to go digital has a price in our society.

Many companies and domains are overwhelmingly analog in their core production processes and likely will stay analog indefinitely. The reasons for this are as varied as the domains and the unique company situation. In many domains and markets, we see some players expanding exponentially while others lag further and further behind due to a lack of agility to perform a digital transformation. In other words, many companies are turning into dinosaurs these days.

Much of the success of new technology comes from startup businesses that dare to think, build, and run in completely different ways than older, larger, and more rigid companies that have already claimed their market share. It is not unusual that such large, established corporations end up buying young, hugely successful companies to obtain their technology and, hence, the advantage they require, for internal or external applications. It is also not unusual for big corporations to lag in innovation in many ways, as they naturally need continuity and robustness to maintain their operations and market share.

As large organizations age, they often settle. The world inside is perceived as stable and secure, and short-term anxiety for the future may erode with time. In some cases, the primary occupation shifts towards stability and continuity, which results in a stronger focus on protecting their products and markets rather than expanding them. By the time employees have been in the same or similar role for a double-digit number of years, the emotion of perceived security may reduce the motivation to make changes beyond the usual, to move outside a given comfort zone, or to take on challenges that involve risks. This is a part of human nature. In many ways, continuity of prosperity is a goal for most throughout their lives. Innovation and great changes may often find more fertile ground in younger and smaller companies with a lower average age of employees, as the openness to change can get reduced with age for people and companies alike. Not until a change becomes imperative for survival and is forced from the outside will many large, old corporations change their approach.

The public sector is another example of a segment of an organization where change is slower to take hold than in the private sector. Of course, it is not always so, but in general, a deep-rooted culture of maintaining the status quo is making it more challenging for public organizations to make rapid changes. I suppose much of the public sector is not expected to win the race to market with innovative digital solutions, as the main focus usually needs to be on the continuity and robustness of services provided to the public.

Clearly, the consequences of trying and failing with new technology are so much larger when our education, health, and wellbeing are at stake than the consequences of trying a new app for browsing online entertainment. The distance between public sector services and online entertainment could perhaps not be greater, as one often cannot afford to take risks through fast innovation while the other cannot afford to take the risk of not engaging in fast innovation.

This is not to say that public sector organizations are always slow to innovate, and private organizations are good at it. Far from it. In some nations, the government makes a point of being agile, fast-paced, and innovative in reaching defined goals across the nation. In January 2018, Lithuania launched Europe's first international blockchain centre[19]. It was the first hub for the digital ledger in the EU. The vision was to help all of Europe connect its blockchain infrastructure more efficiently with the rest of the world. One important driver was the prospect of developing use cases and businesses involving blockchain technology. This move opened up and pushed for several opportunities in the financial market space, where companies like the Bank of Lithuania are offering blockchain-based solutions[20].

---

19   https://www.neweurope.eu/article/lithuania-debuts-eu-gateway-global-blockchain-in-dustry/
20   https://www.lb.lt/en/lbchain

The Estonia-based company Funderbeam[21] is another example. They offer financial services in the area of listing, investments, and fundraising based on blockchain technology. The Estonian government has consciously laid out and enacted a digital strategy to enable financial businesses to thrive in an innovative technology space. Estonia has been able to attract international investment in the area of innovative technology. A thriving tech startup scene for business solutions serving the country was established as a result.

OPENING UP DATASETS

The gap between organizations that innovate efficiently and those that do not is increasing over time. The introduction of 'smart technology' into our world through innovative commercial smart goods has pushed the pace of digital use case innovation towards an exponential curve pointing ever more upwards. This exponential growth of innovation is taking place in parallel with the exponential growth of available data globally. Many consider the exponential growth of data to be the driver of the increased innovation rate. I prefer to see data and innovation as two sides of the same coin: they fuel each other. Increased amounts of data fuel innovation, while innovation fuels new datasets.

The coining of the term 'big data'[22] during the last decade refers to a growing number of datasets that contain an unprecedentedly large amount of data points. Such extremely large datasets have provided unprecedented opportunities for creating digital use cases. The opening up of entirely new, and often huge, datasets made available to the public through the internet mirrors a changing global culture when it comes to data.

Data, as information, is traditionally thought of and treated as property. The trend of opening up new datasets online and making them available for shared use through application programming interfaces (APIs)[23], opens exciting opportunities. The idea that data should be shared whenever possible, is in some ways, revolutionary, as it requires trust between all involved parties to do so. One would not easily put a pot of money on the

---

21   https://www.funderbeam.com/

22   Wiki on big data: Big data is a field that treats ways to analyze, systematically extract information from, or otherwise deal with datasets that are too large or complex to be dealt with by traditional data-processing application software.

23   Wiki on application programming interface: API is a computing interface thatdefines interactions between multiple software intermediaries. It defines the kinds of calls or requests that can be made, how to make them, the data formats that should be used, the conventions to follow, etc.

street for everyone to help themselves. It clearly requires benefits beyond the conventional sale of a product to motivate such behavior.

The early automotive industry provides an early example of how opening up information across a competitive landscape was applied to the common good. The Alliance of Automobile Manufacturers supervised an agreement for cross-licensing patents in the field of car production, which was ratified in 1915[24]. When mass production of such a complex product as a car became mainstream among the manufacturers, it made sense to share certain patents across the major producers. This was to ensure the interchangeability of parts between manufacturers. Mass production required the standardization of components. Focus on the process, combining precision, interchangeability, synchronization, and continuity, were all rapidly increasing so that the manufacturers would benefit from the supply of parts from large-scale part manufacturers. In turn, the customers buying the cars would benefit from easier access to spare parts.

In the 1980s, open-source software gained popularity among a number of software companies. The idea of opening up source code to the public and allowing for the use and modification of code allowed for an efficient and fast evolution of the software. There are many variations in the open-source world today, including varying degrees of licensing and modifications. The idea that software production companies enable their end-users to innovate with the core product freely opens up the possibility for the highest-yielding use cases to become mainstream. The scaling of the most valuable use cases depends on the end-users sharing the innovative code with other end-users freely.

Applying the general principle of sharing across manufacturing patents, software code, and now data, we can observe how the overarching principle of sharing information of any given type can create value for all. Data has become a commodity. The sharing of any new commodity is a daring first step to take, and it requires true visionaries to make the first bold steps. When what is shared is shared by many across a given size of the market, the payback becomes the greatest. If the majority of producers and end consumers do not perceive any or enough value in sharing, the benefits of sharing may fail. No party will reap the benefits.

---

24   https://www.britannica.com/technology/automotive-industry

CONTINUITY AND STABILITY VS. AGILITY AND INTERCHANGEABILITY

If one is uncertain whether an organization is a stayer or a leader in the field of technology innovation, it makes sense to look closer at what exactly the core product or core production line is. A lot of organizations claim to be providing 'breaking-edge technology,' when in fact they are not. Over the years, I believe I have heard a majority of CEOs in tech claim that their company is 'breaking edge' in at least some area. It is needless to say that it is impossible for more than 50% of all companies to work on the cutting edge of technology at any given time. The majority cannot share the lead in the technology race. To me, it shows that most tech companies would like to take the lead in their area, both in terms of market share and technological advances, if they could.

CEOs may also proclaim that they are leading in their field because the image of them being a successful leader sells. For a CEO to openly confess that the company is lagging in the application of innovative technology could potentially cut the CEO's career very short. It would be a marketing disaster for the company. Young, small, agile, and enthusiastic technology startups shout from the rooftops about their right to enter the market and take their share—presenting their true cutting-edge technology to a wider consumer market. This is often the nightmare haunting the more seasoned CEO responsible for a large organization that is harder to change and that is less likely to produce something new and breathtaking in spite of large investments.

Looking at large ERP (enterprise resource planning) software providers, some of them have been global leaders for decades. SAP and Oracle were both founded in the 1970s, and since then they have each maintained a large portion of their respective market segments globally. One great challenge these two companies continuously have to deal with is accommodating their existing customer base by supplying a robust, predictable, and secure solution for a wide range of in-house processes while simultaneously looking modern. SAP and Oracle are challenged by the shift of focus from work processes to data and from proprietary in-house instances to cloud-based product offerings. Both SAP and Oracle are dealing with these challenges reasonably well, yet they are forced to spend large resources accommodating customers that want both secure and stable operations as well as fast and dynamic access to data through interchangeable applications and software.

Many customers have applied SAP and Oracle software across such large parts of their internal operations that it seems their entire backbone relies on these ERP systems. For many, it seems like too much of a challenge to exchange their ERP implementations with cloud-based solutions, or they assume that they need the same high level of security in-house that SAP and Oracle profess to provide. The stability of the applications and the in-house implementation of such ERP solutions are important arguments for many large organizations. Especially those 'locked in' to a state of rigidity and complex internal processes after using the same ERP provider for decades. Many organizations do not know how to get out of such large proprietary installations of ERP applications and move towards lighter cloud-based solutions. SAP, Oracle, and several other ERP providers understand the cemented situation of their client base. One of the consequences is their often-enormous license fees, based on the fact that their customers are stuck with their current ERP system. The cost of change is often considered greater for their clients than the cost of staying with an aging ERP solution.

Companies like SAP and Oracle need to act on market demands, or they will become outdated by smaller, younger ERP cloud-based software suppliers that will take an increasing share of the new customers in the market. In addition, Microsoft 365 is currently pushing hard to widen their corporate market segment in this space with a rapidly growing service offering, now including ERP functionality easily accessible in the cloud. SAP and Oracle are slowly moving their new product offerings into the cloud, as they have to appear innovative and agile in spite of the focus on their long-term client base, which often still uses proprietary software applications.

Traditional ERP providers need to manage this stretch between the client base that has purchased proprietary enterprise-wide ERP installations and the more agile client base that is better prepared to move into the cloud. Both SAP and Oracle are now managing an increasing number of product offerings in the cloud while also trying to maintain many proprietary licenses, simply because they are such good sources of licensing income.

I chose SAP and Oracle as examples because they represent two long-term market leaders that, for now, manage to maintain a still-widening spectrum of client types. On one end they maintain decades-long client relationships requiring stable and secure operations, often expressed through expensive on-site licensing schemes and proprietary enterprise-wide installations. This is sometimes referred to as the customer keeping their own software and hardware in the basement. On the other end of the client base, younger companies are often building their internal operations and processes based on master data modeling, using cloud offerings when they can. The latter is far more agile and capable of interchanging almost any part of their internal processes based on proactive leadership decisions, often taken with cost management and efficiency in mind.

Most other actors in the software market, also outside the crystallized example of ERP, are often forced to put their focus on one type of client. Either the customers are seeking security, stability, and continuity, which require a more conservative approach, or they are a more agile and forward-leaning client base, where innovative and agile solutions are required.

Some may disagree with me on this point and claim that many companies can do both. I suspect that is a massive challenge to undertake. Over the years, I have intermittently worked for a software company that supplies expert systems for a small number of mobile phone operators. Before I would enter any meeting with any of the clients, I would put my SIM card into the brand of phone each mobile phone operator would represent. I would not be seen in any sales meeting using the phone brand of a competitor. This meant that I had to keep a number of mobile phones running in parallel. All my clients knew I was serving several mobile operators. I could very well understand that it was important for each client to observe my loyalty and attention to their specific brand. But I was puzzled and found it odd how much it meant to the client that I was using 'their' model of phone when I was with them. Some of the phones would be more sporty models, and I could easily match my blouse with jeans and sneakers in a client meeting. Later, I could easily swap my jeans for a skirt and some heels if I was using a business-model mobile phone for my next client meeting. To me, this shows how specific the market share and culture of each client can be.

Today, almost 20 years later, I hope that the same clients would prefer to look at whether or not my product offering was in-house proprietary or in the cloud. This now reflects a far greater cultural difference than any clothing or brand flashing could represent. I suspect that some large, conservative, and static software providers are still attempting to bridge image gaps through marketing rather than rebuilding their products to suit changing markets. They portray themselves as modern and agile while, in reality, they try to hide how complex, processing heavy, and outdated their backend technology is.

AWARENESS OF INNOVATION RATE

It is possible to keep track of how mature an organization is when it comes to being innovative. This dictates the capacity to disrupt markets. Management pep talks depicting positive views to employees on how advanced and brilliant the organization is may work to some extent in the short term. In the long term, employee skills and organizational culture will soon reveal whether innovation is real or not. Many organizations are skillfully measuring the competence levels across the organization and using feedback forms to gauge the sentiment and opinions of the employees. 'Management by Objectives'[25] is an established and useful method to get the organization to perform in the desired direction[26].

Besides using goal-oriented tools like 'Management by Objectives' or 'Balanced Scorecard,' which have become increasingly popular over the last few decades, I find it useful to navigate another level of orientation. An encompassing organizational orientation level enables the ability to gauge the maturity of the organization and its place in the current market landscape.

The pace of innovation is both a cause and a result of the state of the current organizational culture. The leadership of any organization will benefit from taking a reality check on the general maturity level of their internal culture and the shared understanding of how innovation can benefit the business side. When the pace of change for product management, service development, and internal functions are looked at realistically, the effort of making the required changes will prove more fruitful. Leadership pep talks may continue and may be very useful for motivation and creating a shared vision for all to aim for, yet the pace of innovation in an organization should be carefully set out to match the pace of change of the people of which the organization consists.

By understanding the internal culture and workings of the organization in comparison with external competition, one can easily see a greater landscape than the managerial, often linear, direction-taking. The conservative direction taken can be observed when a leader makes a statement of what he or she wants, expecting everyone to follow orders

---

25   Early background literature on management by objectives: *A contingency model of leadership effectiveness* by F.E. Fiedler (1954); *Advances in Experimental Social Psychology* by L. Berkowitz; Studies in Leadership by Alvin W. Gouldner (1950).

26   Today the book *Measure What Matters* by John Doerr is commonly read by managers learning how to use Objectives and Key Results (OKRs), a structured approach to goal-setting and decision-making in business.

accordingly. When such an authoritarian approach is used, at least the top management should be knowledgeable and reflective about as many layers in the organization as possible, so that the decisions made by the senior leadership can be as realistic as possible.

In this way, the leadership should bring forward change in the most efficient way by optimizing on the acceleration of innovation according to what the culture can tolerate. To understand where the sweet spot lies within the pace of innovation, a maturity analysis of the various parts and functions within the organization may be performed. A maturity analysis on cultural aspects may also be produced. When this is in place, it will become clearer which tools may be best to work with to achieve the desired pace.

There are various frameworks on human maturity in the field of psychology. Many of these may be applied to organizational settings and used for cultural assessments as well. When the maturity of the organization across specific fields is well described, the choice of frameworks to apply to effectuate change becomes readily available as well.

As an Integral Master Coach™ I have studied a number of frameworks applied to human adult development. I believe more tools from the fields of HR and psychology should be applied in the areas of product management, service development, and organizational change. Maturity levels are reflected in every perspective we are able to take on, whether the dimension is market, product, or internal functions.

I have seen the Myers-Briggs Type Indicator[27] [28] framework successfully applied in team-building training. Consultants gain insight into how teams can work better when referring to personality frameworks. Another popular and more recent framework for working with personality types is the Big Five Personality Traits[29]. Personally, I like to work with the Enneagram of Personality[30] as this framework is rather detailed and also goes into depth regarding paths of development within each personality type. In other words, I personally like this developmental model because it is actionable, contrary to many other personality models. On the other side, the Enneagram of Personality has been criticized due to its complexity and distance from more mainstream psychological models.

---

27   https://www.psychologytoday.com/us/basics/myers-briggs
28   https://en.wikipedia.org/wiki/Myers%E2%80%93Briggs_Type_Indicator
29   https://en.wikipedia.org/wiki/Big_Five_personality_traits
30   https://en.wikipedia.org/wiki/Enneagram_of_Personality

The Maslow Hierarchy of Needs[31] is a well-known model within the field of organizational psychology. I find Maslow's theory a great example of how a model can be applicable on both an individual and organizational level.

Many may not agree with me when I share my view that the most important thing is not which model for human change one chooses to work with. I believe the most important thing is that a choice is made to work with one or more specific models for human development and change. I believe any of the change models I have come across can be adjusted so that they may be applied to organizations and cultures as well as to individuals. I often hear that organizations working with the Big Five Personality Traits are very excited about their internal progress in changing matters. I think this is great and proves that change is possible, but I am hesitant to say that one model is better than another. The important thing is that a model is chosen to work with. I think of models like storage boxes and hooks in a wardrobe. If there are none available, the environment may not be structured and used in a sensible way, as there is no shared agreement as to where things belong. It is more important to choose one system and agree that everyone will use it in the same way than to bicker about which exact system is chosen. One system may fit one organization better than another, and one organization may benefit more from introducing a specific process than what another organization does.

If it is still difficult to understand the maturity of an organization, its type preferences, or its changing pace, this will likely pose a challenge to its leadership. Disconnected leadership or a lack of understanding within the organization are often red flags in a shifting market. An easier and more accessible way to gauge the culture of change could be to measure the current pace of innovation within the organization. By using Questback tools inside and perhaps outside the organization, one can get access to the perceived pace of innovation and make decisions on that basis.

WHERE DOES THE COMPANY EARN ITS MONEY?

It may seem like an obvious question, but there could be a variety of answers that members of the organization may come up with when asked. Even if many answers are variations on a theme, a lack of absolute clarity on the business model can create friction for a new product on the drawing board. Particularly when business models are disrupted by new competition. This is why it makes sense to start with the most basic of questions.

---

31   https://en.wikipedia.org/wiki/Maslow%27s_hierarchy_of_needs

One early lesson of street smarts in business is to follow the stream of money. What are you selling, and who are the customers? Large industrial conglomerates may have several ways and several core processes to earn money. This would easily mean that the understanding of the core product and the core production line varies between different parts of the company. It also means that various parts of the company may experience different maturity levels and levels of preparedness for innovation and disruptive ideas. What may seem like a good and interesting idea to some parts of the conglomerate may seem more like a scare or a threat to other parts of the same organization.

WHO IS THE REAL CUSTOMER?

As we see business models evolve and develop faster than ever in a growing landscape of technical opportunity, it is most important to keep an eye on who the real customer is. Business models are shifting fast, and companies that are used to competing find themselves in situations where the competitors are not the same as a few short years ago.

One example is heavy equipment manufacturers, who until recently operated in a world where all competition could be defined as mechanical equipment manufacturing in some way or another. An increasing number of customers expect mechanical equipment to be connected to the internet. This results in heavy equipment manufacturers finding themselves in a situation where they are competing directly with software companies as the introduction of software applications and services adds to the original mechanical piece.

The end-user is no longer exclusively the analog factory operator. The software engineer optimizing the use of each piece of heavy equipment is now an important customer. The customer base for many products has shifted drastically in a relatively short time and companies are still trying to find their bearings in the client landscape.

How well defined is the core production line and what is the nature of it?

In general, companies know their core product, their core production line, and who their real customer is. Stating anything else would simply be arrogance. Still, evolving markets place companies in a situation where some don't fully understand the nature and characteristics of the current dynamics. To be more nuanced, at times, not all employees at every level of the organization understands the nature of the business the company is in.

In parallel to evolving markets, the core production line and product may be unclear to employees in some of the organizational layers. The better every level of the organization understands the core of the business and its nature, the more likely every level is to understand the organizational capacities as well as its relevance in the market. It is particularly important that the leadership has a clear idea of how the core business is aligned with organizational capacities, as it is their job to communicate this to the company. The coherence of the organization can improve drastically when every party and level have a shared understanding of what the product, production line, and nature of the organization are all about. When the competitive landscape shifts and business models evolve, this shared understanding becomes crucial.

One example is that it is possible for a logger working in the forest to perceive the work process and production line as mostly analog if the high-tech use cases are kept at the sawmill and not applied in the logging process. Some parts of the organization may look at the nature of a production line and assume that the rest of the company works at the same level of complexity. If the logger is not informed about the complexity of the production line taking place in the sawmill, there is little chance for the logger to optimize each trunk being prepared for transport in a way that may support the process in the sawmill.

Such challenges have been considered a 'process improvement' issue by many for a long time. I suspect at least part of the resolution could be in the shared understanding of the greater value chain by all personnel involved. When a greater context is introduced for all and the nature of the task is well defined, it makes it easier to accept changes to the details. The overall benefits may be better communicated and understood by various stakeholders in a larger value chain.

A window glazier may consider his core trade to be glazing, while the extra added value of providing burglar-secure window solutions adds value to the services and products. Another company providing similar services and products may place itself in the anti-theft security business, while glazing is a spin-off.

Such companies may end up targeting different market segments, using different market strategies, and striving for different in-house skills depending on the outlook for the core product and core production line. All companies are unique, and for most organizations, it makes sense to understand exactly what perspective to take on the core product. The organization can be unified across all units and departments with a shared vantage point on who the customer is and what the core product is. Clear communication of this shared view can ensure that the right competencies are recruited and the exact market segment targeted. The growing digital complexity of anti-theft systems will disrupt the organization and shift the skills required to fulfill this additional service for what started as a glazing firm. When digital disruption shifts the market, companies need to change their narratives internally as well as externally.

Many innovative organizations are letting go of this exact view of what the core product and production line look like for the benefit of agile and dynamic product and service development. It can seem necessary to let go of what is old and existing, taking a leap of faith to invite new ideas and innovation to emerge more freely. Sometimes this approach works if the intentional lack of steering is allowed for a defined period of time and for a defined part of the organization. Close oversight and cost control are usually needed. In the case of extraordinary organizations, it may also work for a longer period, and newly defined values may be gained. Such a lack of steering can turn things askew, though. Time and resources are spent on vague business cases, and if innovation happens, it does not necessarily apply to any crucial part of the core product or the core production line. Another danger can be optimistic reporting from the development team on the expected product and value creation. This can postpone optimal decision-making that is needed early on to prevent loss of value.

Many companies tend to start applying new technologies like ML and IoT to non-essential supportive processes and functions in the organization. A prime example already visited is how chatbots are introduced in customer service, which is considered a soft and easy place to start experimenting with new technology. It is often easier to introduce a chatbot in the customer care process than it is to introduce ML with advanced algorithms in bottleneck situations in the core production line. In this case, the flip side of easily accessible innovation is lower-value creation from innovation. Most of the time, the benefits of finding the right bottleneck in the production line and working efficiently with datasets of any kind to resolve real human problems will be far more valuable in the long run. Important production line datasets will yield an entirely different ROI than any peripheral use case introduced because it was the easier course to start with.

More often than not, use cases will prove themselves to be far more valuable when applied where it matters most and with a thorough understanding of the in-house core product and core business. Use cases applied on the outskirts off where the core value is created will probably create far less value in the long run. Aim for the most valuable use cases straight away without spending valuable time and resources far away from where the real value creation happens. If the use case does not work as intended, the learning will also become proportionally greater for all when it happens at the core of the company's value creation and close to the crucial action.

HOW MATURE IS YOUR DIGITAL KNOWLEDGE LEVEL?
One dimension explained for use case development is to gauge digital competence across the organization. Sometimes a few will have strong digital competencies, while many have less. Other times, digital skillsets are spread more widely across various parts of the organization. It does matter whether digital knowledge is spread across the organization or not. It may seem sufficient that a minority has the deep digital skills needed for a given use case, as long as they are the right people in the right place.

Still, in larger organizations, the amount of red tape, elaborate supportive processes, and activity evolving outside the core product and production process may hamper the traction of any high-tech use case substantially. If the organization does not have a digitally mature culture company-wide, the resistance and lack of traction for digital use cases may suffocate any real digital initiatives before they are fully developed. This is about change management as well as how every piece of the organizational puzzle performs according to locally set expectations. If a function in the organization is set to work analog, then that function may soon become the weakest part of the value chain that is required to work seamlessly to make a digital use case succeed.

Think of a food production plant that provides freshly packed produce. There are many food manufacturers that are in the process of developing and applying digital sensor systems in food packaging[32] that can detect

---

32   An example of a company providing digital sensor technologies for food freshness is inno-scentia.com. Examples of companies working on embedding the expiration date of each food item in the packaging barcode are beepscan.com and deligate.app.

the freshness of the produce within. By applying a small digital solution to each food packaging container, the freshness of the produce as well as an expected expiration date may be dynamically displayed on the packaging. This invention has the potential to reduce food waste substantially as well as assure both the producing company, the supply chain, and the end customer about the current quality of the produce at any given time after the perishables leave the production plant. It is a prerequisite that the packaging department at the plant has a thorough understanding of the value of this new digital component. Without an appropriate understanding of the components, functions, and value each sensor provides for a package, it may become a challenge for the company to get the packaging department to handle the technology appropriately. The effect could be a reduced accuracy of the digital sensor units after packaged items leave the plant.

Another hypothetical example may be simpler. If mail delivery had the possibility of understanding the unique fragility of each parcel delivered, it would spend the exact amount of effort needed for each parcel to be delivered as safely and promptly as possible. The balance between quality, efficiency, and cost could be monitored and optimized along the entire value chain of mail delivery. This could increase both the speed with which each parcel could be delivered as well as reduce breakage to a minimum. But for such a hypothetical solution to work, every part of the supply chain involved would have to be knowledgeable about the use case, understand it, and adjust their behavior accordingly. If only one person did not understand and ended up handling a parcel roughly to save time, some of the benefit of the use case would soon be lost.

THE TRADITIONAL PACE OF CHANGE FOR AN ORGANIZATION

In general, large organizations that have been around for some time are often more challenged with implementing rapid changes than younger, smaller organizations. The latter are often accustomed to a faster pace of change as a prerequisite for survival in highly competitive market situations. Here are some good questions to ask any employee or leader regarding a company's pace of change:

- How long does it take the organization to restructure a medium-sized department internally?
- How long does it take the organization to develop a new product, from the very start of any planning to the very end when the product is available (on the shelf)?
- How long is the average life cycle of products or services produced by

the company? In other words, for how long do products last before customers need to substantially update or exchange them?

These are far from absolute determinants regarding company culture and capacity for change. Still, the three questions mentioned above provide an indication of whether this is an organization that is hard to turn around or capable of turning on its axis quickly and on short notice. There is no denying that any cruise ship with 5,000+ passengers takes much longer to turn around than a Formula 1 powerboat. Size matters.

There are many other factors that influence the acceleration of technological change in organizations, product management, or service development. When leadership recognizes this challenge and understands the reasons behind it, then change becomes easier to navigate, resolve, and accelerate. Then adaptation can happen at the right level, be it strategic, tactical, or operational.

The changing pace of innovation can bring not-so-obvious challenges, with one's focus often placed where it should not be. For instance, it can be challenging to try to figure out when marketing innovation should be more aggressive or if it is more valuable to put innovation efforts into product management or service development. Solutions to problems that may arise during increased acceleration of innovation may be found across several areas; it is of great importance for leadership to recognize where these problems may arise and, if they exist at all, before optimal solutions can be found. Various changes may be required across various business areas and various products. Other times, it may be valuable to accelerate and gain momentum, getting buy-in from stakeholders to succeed. When leadership can prioritize the pace of innovation correctly within the organization, it is more likely that it will benefit all involved.

The *nature of the business* and the *specific market segments* may not only influence the change pace of an organization, but these two factors will often set the absolute conditions under which any given business, product, or service exists. If a media company does not deliver a given gaming product to market in time, it could result in another competing business bringing another innovative gaming product to market, which could quickly take over the market share. Here we can see how *time to market* for a new product is crucial. On the other end of the scale, we find reduced-fat milk or your local online yellow pages. These market segments and audiences will, for the most part, stay the same, and the products are not naturally fast-changing. Providing a quality product, and in the case of the yellow pages, an updated product, is more important than reinventing and changing the product. In many cases, the qualities of consistency and continuity reflect on the production organization too. I struggle to come up with examples where the pace of a particular business differs from the pace of its products and services. If the market is dynamic, companies are often agile and able to change quickly. A more stable market with strong stability and continuity for the demand of a product or service allows companies to become more set in their ways.

If there were any indication as to which companies are better suited and prepared for fast-paced market changes, my approach would often be to look at the company's history and marketplaces. Has the company been agile and well adapted to disruptive changes in market conditions at any time before? If so, in what way has it been dynamic, and how did it overcome external changes? If the organization has not dealt with drastic changes in conditions earlier or has not done so successfully, it could be wise to consider the establishment of a satellite organization apart from the company to deal with the disruption at hand. This is valid advice regardless of whether the nature of the disruption is internal or external. If the market requires changes to a product or if an internal supply chain challenge disrupts the production line, both external and internal challenges will likely require a new way of thinking to resolve new problems. Well-considered ad hoc groups may be a good start when aiming to create new ways to resolve new challenges. Entire new teams built outside the existing organization may work even better when agile and dynamic approaches are required to deal with disruptions.

I have heard of spearheading[33] referred to as a way of introducing new concepts into large and seemingly static companies. By looking for any part of the organization that is already more open to change than the rest, it is possible to test out the development of new concepts internally. It can even be less important which department or team this may be, as long as its members are competent and display the characteristics of openness and curiosity. If the department of housekeeping in an office building has independently and successfully introduced the use of cleaning robots, then it could be that these people are the right ones to check in with and ask how training of production personnel may be done in the best possible way when introducing production robots. The housekeeping department may have experiences to share, for instance, a discovery that, in a highly

---

33   https://grammarist.com/usage/spearhead/

mechanical or service-oriented company, the organization in general has a lower level of digital competence than first perceived. The first step of general PC training may be made available to all to prepare for future digitization projects. It could also be that the housekeeping department is a good place to start another digitization project, such as the introduction of handheld units for digital reporting of work processes. Then it could also be useful to harvest simple observations that could be overlooked, for instance, that the placement of power outlets in the building is not optimized for charging stations in a more digital work landscape where digital equipment may need frequent charging. By carefully selecting any existing team that can already show positive results from self-initiated digitalization, the company may be able to share digital experiences through a well-placed pilot and encourage a more widely shared positive attitude towards future digitalization.

It is not uncommon for large, slow, and rather set organizations to establish 'Big Hairy Audacious Goals[34]' (BHAG) of becoming a fast-moving, agile organization capable of turning things around in a short amount of time. Usually, this is an impossible request from top management for many reasons. Sometimes the intention is to manage a short stint where the goal is to create a much-needed, faster output. Such stints, if pushed over longer periods of time, may lead to increased turnover of personnel, decreased quality in products and services, as well as overall organizational fatigue. The large cruise ship is simply not built to move like a Formula 1 powerboat. It will creak until things start breaking if put under pressure. To continue the boat metaphor, it is important to recognize what type of vehicle the top management is leading and optimize accordingly. If this basic principle is not followed, the organization may risk a further significant slowdown in the long run, as well as a small or large breakdown of in-house personnel, culture, and equipment. It could easily result in a confused, tired, and left-behind organization. This is before mentioning the searing costs as a consequence.

I love the stories from some of my New Zealand friends who work on sailboats. Some of their clients want to order boats that are simply impossible to build. They want the fastest, highest-performance boat on the water, and at the same time, they want the comforts of a large, wide-body boat. No matter what the vehicle is, it is simply a contradiction to be simultaneously the fastest and the largest. The boat can be slim and

---

34   The term was coined in the book *Built to Last: Successful Habits of Visionary Companies* by Jim Collins and Jerry Porras.

fast in the water or rounded with a bigger belly containing comfortable furnishings that build more drag in the water. To go fast, volume and width need to be reduced compared to length.

There are a few select organizations that are both large and can embrace fast changes. These are unique organizations that are highly specialized in their area. One example would be NGOs like the Red Cross and Care. They can build refugee camps for thousands of people in challenging conditions in a matter of days. These are highly specialized operational cases, and it is important to remember the few select KPIs these NGOs are aiming for. Basic safety, shelter, waste disposal, food, and water for as many as possible in a short period of time are often the drill. After that, the rules of the game change when it comes to operating a refugee camp. This is an entirely different task than building one. No organization can specialize in everything they do in every field, both internally and externally. To gain the swiftness of a fast-moving vehicle, a few select targets are needed, as well as the willingness to let go of a whole lot of bulge.

Another area where the balance between speed, effect, and quality is at the center is project management. Best practices state that the ideal balance between the three parameters of cost, time, and quality required for an agreed delivery is crucial for any seasoned project manager. There is no way for any organization or company to avoid this balancing act. The conditions directing the pace of innovation in any organization cannot stay constant if the speed of change is to be accelerated. In the human dimension, there is a popular expression used to state this balance of relationships: 'Something's gotta give'.

DO TECH PARTNERS UNDERSTAND THE NEED FOR CHANGE?
When a company aims for a position in the market, there are usually dependencies on partner companies in one or more forms. Raw materials, parts, production equipment, external supply chains, temporary workforces, logistics, and sourcing are only a few examples of the various types of suppliers and providers that are increasingly turning into tech partners in some form or another. The value chain of a finished product is often longer and more complex than it was a few decades ago. Most large supply chains and value chains today are already globally digitalized and optimized to various degrees. The understanding of what value chains can be beyond the internal organization, or should be, remains a continuous exploration for many.

Diagram 6

Enablers for New Business Models

Enablers for new business models are the same as the enablers
for exponential innovation in tech.

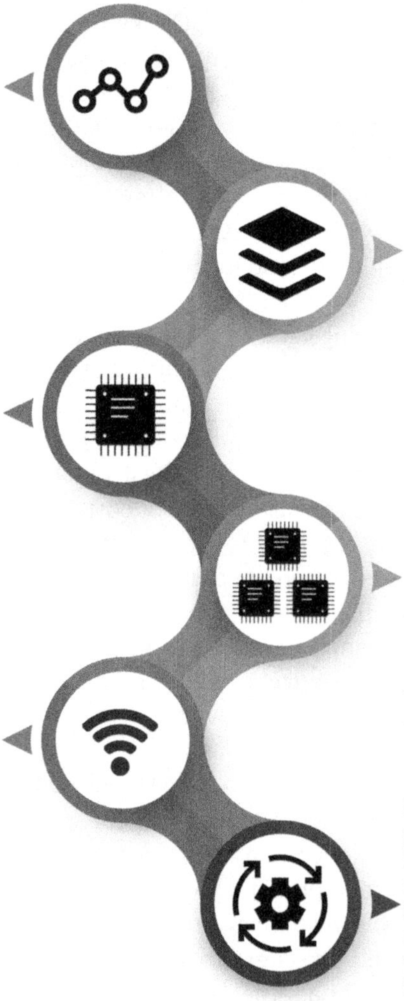

More data points:
The amount of data points available is increasing exponentially, not only due to the introduction of new data sets, but overall due to the amount of data harvested globally increasing exponentially, simply because it is possible and because data in itself has become a greater commodity than ever before.

New data sets:
A fast-growing number of types of data available globally is the result of the recent increase in possibilities for harvesting data.

Cheaper hardware and sensor technology:
An overall reduction in price per HW unit in recent years has accelerated consumer access to increasingly large volumes of HW and sensor technologies.

More hardware and sensor technology:
In recent years, increased volumes of HW and sensor technologies have been made available to the consumer market due to rapidly increasing demand.

Higher connectivity speed:
Exponential increases in connectivity speeds available to the consumer market (3G, 4G, and 5G accessibility) make it increasingly feasible to connect more datasets and larger amounts of data globally.

Higher processing power:
Exponential improvements in the performance of digital electronics over many years are steadily hitting the consumer market.

* HW (hardware)
* ST (sensor tech)

When it comes to partners, one important question to ask is: *What part of any external value chain can be influenced by the organization?* It can initially seem easier to influence incoming, which means upstream, value chains. This indicates digitizing functional areas like procurement, supply chain with raw materials, and parts. Digitizing outgoing, which means downstream value chains, would look different and involve different parts of the organization. When a product or service leaves the premises, it may appear more challenging for many to exercise control over what happens next. After this point of exit, it's a typical digitalization move to provide more smart app capability, frequently at no cost to users, in order to increase control.

So many consumer goods, ranging from coffee machines to cars, are delivered with smartphone apps as part of the product or maintenance service. The benefit for manufacturing companies varies depending on whether they gain new datasets on utilization, customer behavior, demographics, and many other datasets. These may be used to optimize the product itself, improve the supply chain, enhance market strategies, or influence end-user behavior directly. Note that these datasets are not merely a market advance compared to older, more established competition. In some domains, the added software makes up a substantial extension of the original value chain and becomes increasingly important compared to the original product or service.

Such shifts in value chains may be disruptive and change the competitive landscape in a short amount of time. One example would be the software offerings on training appliances in gyms. While older motorized treadmills should, in theory, do the job just fine, a lot of gym-goers may prefer the treadmill that offers an app for program adaptation and planning for an optimized personal training program. The treadmill recognizes the person through a connected personal smartphone. By collecting historical data from former training sessions, a range of customized training programs may be offered in real-time. The app may be integrated with a Fitbit, a sleeping cycle app, or a nutrition app to optimize the experience for gym users further.

Such an app could potentially disrupt the market for personal trainers locally, or it may work in the opposite way by encouraging some gym-goers to hire a personal trainer. Innovative solutions can sometimes be disruptive in unknown ways or may shift in unexpected ways. Disrupting markets by substantially changing value chains is often an act of balance.

There could be unforeseen risks associated with disrupting an existing market share beyond what the innovation was intended to do.

In this example of adding a smart app to a treadmill, there are several markets that could be disrupted. First, the market for treadmills may be affected by the offering. Gyms may turn around quickly and prefer to lease new treadmills topped up with smart apps to retain and gain gym-goers. Second, gym-goers may download their own suitable smart training apps and integrate their use with the tech in the treadmill. Sometimes the personal Fitbit beats the integrated smart app of the treadmill. Third, the personal trainer may need to come up with something even smarter and better than either of the smart apps. An example could be to offer alternative outdoor training sessions that remove the focus entirely from tech innovation by offering an alternative non-digital service. There may be many other disruptive elements taking place in the case of the smart treadmill, yet it is a challenge for any party to gain a complete overview of the disruptive potential before the innovation is developed, tested, and applied in the market.

Organizations aiming to innovate with tech usually discuss in great detail the degrees of disruption and the desired versus undesirable consequences when use cases are developed.

At times, perspectives on the innovation speed of partners can disrupt value chains or entire markets. If an entire market segment of partners is considered to be lagging or leading in comparison with the internal organization of a company, this leads to proactive choices around value chains and supply chains. For instance, if a given type of supplier is lagging in the application of tech innovation when the consumer market requires an increased rate, a company may be forced to make changes to the core product.

One type of partnership that is heavily affected by technology disruption is that of the suppliers of raw materials for production lines. The quality of the incoming raw materials as well as the quality of the supply chain may be monitored in detail and in real-time today in a way that was hard to imagine only a few years ago. Digital records of quality controls on raw materials are often expected at several points or continuously before raw materials reach the production site.

One hypothetical example could be a furniture manufacturer who may be challenged to obtain the right quality of leather for upholstering. The digital tracking of the supply chain and industry-standard quality certifications of certain wool fabrics could, for instance, be more advanced than in the leather industry. The furniture manufacturer could be forced to use more wool fabrics for upholstering due to a growing, environmentally conscious end-user segment. Environmentally savvy consumers are actively demanding industry certification of raw material origins and also natural renewable materials when purchasing consumer goods.

It is worthwhile to notice that in some cases the absence of innovative tech solutions may be a market advantage. Supermarkets providing non-genetically modified produce is a stellar example of when the absence of tech innovation is a benefit in a given market segment.

Following this thread of logic, one can see how the disruption of value chains has huge impacts on the landscape of partnerships. New partners may need to be involved, for instance, software development partners who provide the appropriate app solution to offer end-users what used to be analog products. What used to be solely commodities in the past are increasingly provided as commodities, including software functionality. Many end-users today expect or prefer to have an app for monitoring the final commodity product. Innovative technology may be seen as a market opportunity for companies to accommodate the needs of the end-user. In other cases, innovative technology may be seen as an opportunity to gain control of an expanding part of an existing value chain. By focusing on the value and where in the value chain the impact may be the strongest, companies can consciously work their way towards digital disruption of the product, production environment, market, or all three.

It varies how various types of companies are prepared for innovation. Every company is unique in culture, organization, and market space. Still, there are some simple general observations that may indicate whether a company will be able to disrupt markets. Often, each company is constructed and wired to work well in a given set of circumstances. While some organizations are built to withstand the endurance of time and global change, others are constructed to be far more dynamic and even short-lived for a reason.

Traditional companies built for robustness and continuity are often the most challenged by market drivers disrupting the competitive landscape. The top management can be eager to prove that it is agile and dynamic in an ever-changing market. Marketing campaigns can foster a global image of a modern, dynamic, and open organization, while in reality, not much new is happening. The diligence of an old organization is simply not environmentally fit for dynamic innovation. Concern about robustness and safety is not encouraging internal disruption.

On the other side, there are lean and agile organizations that are prepared for change. They focus on the ability to make internal changes according to external market situations. Control mechanisms are fewer and often not overly complicated, yet well-placed. For such organizations, it is culturally important to excel and drive the market with innovative concepts. Dynamic action and reaction are clues. One is focused on maintaining the known, while the other is focused on exploring beyond what has been tried. In short, these two extremes of a company model are differently prepared for innovation and the application of disruptive tech.

If there is any place between these two extremes where there is space for innovation, I would look for robust yet *light* organizations that are very well aware of their internal and external strengths and weaknesses. These companies may deliberately target the sector or section of their value chain where innovation should occur while also understanding how disruption should take place. For stable, robust organizations, there is always a price to pay when going light by removing complex processes and aiming for agility, but when doing so in a limited part of the organization, it might work. It is important to observe how existing *heavy* processes may limit the speed of what could become disruptive innovation and take appropriate action when needed. The moment an outdated or extensive process comes down on any innovative project, progress and speed will be hampered. The ambition of what is possible will be lowered to fit into the existing organization.

If innovation is to be achieved efficiently, it is important that top management is clear regarding *what* and *who* is to be progressive and innovative. It could be part of the product, part of the core production line, or a market disruption through reform and change. But not all of it simultaneously, because then innovation would be deprived of 'oxygen'. If a progressive flame is to be kept alive in a conservative environment, it needs to be carefully observed and nurtured. The direct environment needs to be changed to facilitate innovation. Only when targeted measures are made to accommodate innovation will an entirely new product in a traditional environment stand any chance of succeeding.

As a contradiction, there may also be young, innovative, and agile organizations that successfully produce robust products and services. Insight and understanding of exactly where robustness and continuity are needed are required. This could be in a part of the organization, in the core production line, or in the product or service itself. What matters is that it is known and accepted in the organization, from top management to domain experts, exactly where robustness and continuity should be aimed. A global, robust approach could quench the agility of the company itself. Top management needs to be aware and awake as to what parts should be agile, fast-paced, and dynamic, while robustness and continuity are secured only where they are needed.

I have seen no definite answers as to which organizations may be best equipped for fast-paced changes. As a rule of thumb, long-established organizations and businesses should look at their history to see when either processes, people and their skill sets, or the products and services changed too quickly for any reason, internal or external. If this has never been observed in the lifetime of the company and it is a well-established company with stable markets, then one could assume that a fast pace of innovation could be difficult to achieve. If the company is young and still considered moldable when it comes to people, processes, products, and services, then change could be easier to achieve in general. Some may consider the age and skillsets of the majority of employees as an important indication as to whether fast change is possible or not.

In my view, nothing influences the pace of innovation in an organization more than the market it operates in. A sad yet valid example of external factors requiring a fast change is the outbreak of war. Markets could be disrupted, and the demand for some products and services may fall drastically while the demand for new products soars. I suspect some textile manufacturers in England noticed such an abrupt change during the Second World War, when the demand for blind curtains increased as London was bombed by the German Air Force. During the same war, German engineering companies like Bosch and Siemens managed to innovate their product lines, adapting to the new world situation by becoming large producers of war-related products. Let's look at the example of Bosch, who invented and started mass production of the spark plug in 1902. The expanding market for automobiles in the decades leading up to the Second World War surely was a factor in the growth and innovation of this engineering company. For Siemens, the production of light bulbs and electronic products had provided expansive growth in the years leading up to 1945. When times changed with the outbreak of war, both Bosch and Siemens managed to turn their operations largely towards war-related products. Both the use of forced labor and the rapidly expanding market for weapons were enablers for Bosch and Siemens to make the fast product changes required to thrive in a disrupted market. It is important to note that market disruption is rarely a story of morale, but rather a story of financial interests driven by events and underpinned by enablers.

AI DRIVING SYSTEMIC SHIFTS

The introduction of AI has changed form and momentum over the last 20 years. From the 1940s to the 1980s, much of the automation introduced consisted of replacing a human task with a machine performing the same, or a very similar, task. With the introduction of IoT and big data, tech innovation has in many ways moved away from the work floor and become far more influential in the boardrooms, where strategic decisions are being made for the entire enterprise. The current disruption is targeted more at business models than at making the task of an individual worker more efficient or safer.

One example is Amazon. Amazon has replaced a vast number of bookstores across the world, as well as the need for booksellers and shop clerks who used to work in smaller independent bookstores. Looking at the disruption Amazon has brought to retail, there are several potential parts of its value chain that may be discussed. I am amazed at how Amazon gives individual customers exactly what they need, both before and after a book is purchased. The way Amazon is applying AI in the form of algorithms that crunch end-user datasets to provide highly customized ads to each potential customer online is superbly sophisticated. Amazon may internally discuss the possibility of speeding up the moment of purchase. Imagine any shop clerk in a bookstore securing the sale of a book to a customer not 15 minutes after the customer enters the shop but perhaps within mere seconds. In an analog world, such potential is hard to grasp, and it clearly shifts the entire business of book shops. This prospect also shifts the required skills to handle the business.

This business model has shifted right before our eyes. The customer is no longer buying the experience of going to a local bookstore, browsing through some shelves, and interacting with the clerk. The move of the bookstore to online premises is perhaps the largest shift Amazon has introduced, but there are other subsequent shifts taking place too, all facilitated by the online experience. The current vending practice is to allow highly customized algorithms to predict the customer's preferences and choices, as well as the speed with which those choices will be made. A few customized individual offers are made to the online customer, and with one-click functionality, the purchase is made and the transaction is secured. This is about the ease of shopping from home. It is also about having the product supplier literally make a choice for the customer by instantly providing highly tailored options.

Twenty-five years ago, the introduction of a PC in the bookstore meant less work for the shop clerk, as the shop staff or the customer could search the database for a book title or author and then find the shelf where the book was situated. This part of digitalization reduced the need for staffing in bookstores while causing little disruption to the business as a whole. The introduction of AI by Amazon was disruptive on a systemic level because a large number of physical bookstores were replaced by one online bookstore. The commercial approach towards each potential online customer became incredibly targeted through the application of AI.

The shift from selling books to adding many other consumer goods to its marketplace was brief for Amazon because datasets of the browsing history of any potential customer were available. The pre-existing process of making book purchases in a physical shop is history for many. The business model has shifted from including competent personal advice from skilled shop clerks to a market-driven data model that pushes customized products to individuals through AI. Today, the online customer is an asset. Browsing the history datasets of each potential customer is also an important asset. The skillset of the shop clerk is still important, but it is now embedded in a larger digital system that is sharper at aiming for a fast sale to any potential customer. Data as a driver has skewed the entire business. An entirely new set of rules as to how the business should work has been established. These new rules aim at increasingly fast purchasing processes that were never such a central issue for most bookstores in the past.

I do not believe that the need for domain expertise will diminish with the introduction of AI. The need for physical presence and personal assistance when looking for a book in a store may be history. Yet, the need for nuanced knowledge about books, cataloging, and categorizing, as well as knowledge about the content of the books themselves, will not go away. When the book business is disrupted, the clerk's domain expertise cannot be entirely replaced by digitalization. The domain expertise on books may be embedded in software tools, including AI, but the need for this domain expertise in the first place has not faded. The untrained attendant in the bookstore who does not hold any specific expertise is the first person to be replaced by technology, while there will always be a need for insight given by domain experts. Solutions, including AI, may be data-driven, but domain expertise cannot be emitted from digital systems. This means that the digital expertise Amazon holds will always be in addition to the bookstore domain expertise that is now embedded in the online system.

Even after decades of digital work automation, there is still a persistent concern that humans will be supplanted by digital technology. The introduction of digital tools and robots was the first and perhaps easiest step to digital transformation. When looking a bit closer, we see that it is manual labor and repetitive tasks that have been replaced by machines. Factory automation has been evolving for two centuries globally, and it has changed the world as we know it. One of the biggest changes is that unskilled labor has been replaced by machines, while more people are relying on education, skills, and insight than ever before to make a living. The larger part of the global population is increasingly becoming more educated. Much of the middle class depends on a trade, profession, or craft and expertise to make a living. The shift during the last few decades has been the increasing degree of digitalization of value chains, adding to the already automated processes and tasks. Digital skills are increasingly becoming the norm for almost any trade, profession, or domain.

The big difference over the last few decades is that domain expertise itself is embedded in digital solutions. The need for domain expertise has never disappeared, although often the required number of domain experts has decreased as the expertise is now increasingly kept in digital systems. The emotional notion of IT engineers taking over the jobs of domain experts is not entirely true. IT engineers are now required in addition to domain experts.

Digitization and digitalization are continuously disrupting and shifting the landscape for a large number of domain experts. It is important to pay attention to how this shift is a result of the changed business models, disrupted work processes, and changed market segments that digital innovation opens up. This shift is usually not the result of technological innovation itself but rather the consequence of a systemic shift in the entire business. The need for skilled labor may be replaced to some extent by digital automation tools, while the need for detailed domain expertise will not go away, as this needs to be embedded in digital systems as well as updated and maintained.

A natural follow-up question is what will happen to domain experts when deep learning is introduced. So far, my observation is that the business models are shifting more than anything else. Domain experts are still needed to embed expertise in digital systems, but as the market changes quickly and disruption of value chains happens more frequently, the domains of expertise are also changing accordingly.

Twenty years ago, a car mechanic spent far more time on analog tasks requiring solely mechanical expertise than she does today. Today, most mechanics spend more time testing digitally for errors, often replacing entire components instead of just fixing the broken part. Each component is likely to have so much expert functionality embedded digitally that it is impossible to fix the component locally. This means that the car manufacturers and their suppliers now own and influence a far greater part of the value chain for the maintenance of cars than before. There is still a need for car mechanics, yet the shift in its business model, enabled by the embedded domain expertise in digital systems, results in extended value chain ownership for the car manufacturer and part supplier. The digitally embedded domain expertise in each component secures the extended value chain of the car manufacturer and part manufacturer. At the same time, it sidelines much of the traditional mechanic's skills.

Digital technology embedded in components still needs domain expertise while the ownership of this expertise has become centralized. The car mechanic keeps the job while the tasks are reduced to testing and replacing components.

From the outside, it may look like the embedded domain expertise in the manufacturer's system, together with the digitalization of each component, is driving the shift in expertise required from the mechanic. In reality, it is the business model of the extended value chain of the manufacturer that is the driver for the change in the mechanic domain expertise.

VALUABLE TAKEAWAYS WHEN INNOVATING

Today, most organizations need to enter into technology partnerships to be able to develop valuable use cases. They could, for instance, be driven by the need to use open APIs to gain access to external datasets, or they could be as fundamental as making a choice for which data platform technology to use enterprise-wide. Many are currently deciding whether to use the cloud, hybrid cloud, or proprietary cloud according to security demands related to their business.

In the past, the greatest challenge when entering into tech partnerships was often the containment and separation of data. Each ERP system, or any other enterprise-wide proprietary system, would be installed with one or more instances in-house. The challenge down the road in applying in-house solutions is the extraction of datasets in useful formats for applying data in other settings. Proprietary datasets have been locked in 'silos' and are challenging to understand in any larger context than the original ERP or enterprise system, where the data is literally buried. Cloud solutions and big data are opening up limitless possibilities for contextualizing (or layering) data in new ways across software instances and enterprises. The global sharing of data has become an ideal in itself in systems where data can be processed and contextualized freely. The sharing of data facilitates rapid change and the rapid development of what used to be complex IT solutions.

That said, it is as important as ever to be cautious about being locked into technology. In place of keeping all data proprietary, or 'in the basement', as the expression goes, one is far better off accessing data from in-house IT systems as well as from the cloud. It is possible to mix and match with data contextualization in easy-entry dashboards on any PC connected to the internet. Business intelligence dashboards based on in-house data warehouses or global data platforms are increasingly the new fad. This does not mean that one cannot get locked in by software vendors and cloud providers anymore. It simply means that being locked in may look a bit different than before. It could also mean being locked out of data access in the cloud for periods of time if any part of the network goes down.

Unforeseen and long-lasting effects could result from choosing one IT cloud provider or partner over another. If we look at the current most important cloud providers in the Western Hemisphere, Google Cloud, Apple, MS Azure, and AWS, it becomes clear that there are differences and limitations between each of them. It can make sense to choose one cloud provider enterprise-wide if one ventures into the cloud, but it makes sense to investigate the pros and cons thoroughly before closing the deal. The cloud provider will probably set some conditions in stone when a solution is chosen. A good architect and business analyst may be one of the most valuable investments before committing to a cloud provider. There could be many factors in need of scrutiny before going all in. Here is a list of example questions that may need to be raised, though the list is far from exhaustive:

- What are the models and limitations of data taxonomies in the cloud platform? Does the organization require a strict and rigid data modeling tool or one that can easily be changed and tuned over a longer period of time?
- Where are the actual data centers of the cloud provider? Will your enterprise-wide data be kept in your country or will it be exported outside your legislative area? Is this important for the organization? Don't forget to ask about the backup locations.
- How are the performance and quality levels of the services provided compared to the processing speed required by the different parts of your enterprise?
- Is it a goal in itself to share current in-house data externally, with the entire world, or with some defined tech partners? What are the reasons for moving to the cloud, and what are the reasons to limit the use of the cloud?
- Does the organization have a strong master data strategy? Is data ownership clear and planned for when moving services into the cloud?
- Is the enterprise planning to move internal services into the cloud? Or parts of the core product in the form of software? Is there a plan to optimize internal operations by making use of cloud technology?
- Does the organization harbor the right skills and sufficient competence to derive value from moving into the cloud? If not, what are the benefits of doing so?
- What will the long-term maintenance and security issues be?
- What is the plan for maintaining the cloud solution? Is the IT department appropriately prepared for going into the cloud, or is the move a strategic goal in itself, perhaps without sufficient substance and thought behind the intended value creation expected from the move?
- Does the use of data platforms fit into the cloud strategy?
- Is there enough shared insight about the differences between private clouds, public clouds, hybrid clouds, and multi-clouds to make good decisions on cloud partner(s)?
- Is there enough shared insight about the pros and cons of various

cloud computing services: infrastructure-as-a-service (IaaS), platform-as-a-service (PaaS), and software-as-a-service (SaaS)?

These are just examples of questions that need to be answered before marrying a tech partner in the cloud. There may be huge advantages to moving into the cloud and using data platforms, yet one of the most important questions to explore upfront is the practicality of changing the cloud (service) provider at a later point in time. Would this be considered an easy or complex task? To get good answers, both a solid master data strategy and a cloud strategy should form the basis for the answers.

It is senseless to get out of a locked-in data situation in an outdated ERP system just to move into another locked-in (or locked-out) data situation where an external partner decides the circumstances. The same conundrum goes for exchanging an in-house data warehouse solution with an external cloud partner, who may lower prices in exchange for long-term contracts that would be challenging to exit. Partner candidates should not be more challenging to exchange, or interchange, than absolutely necessary. External providers can set the conditions for your data management. They can also move you from an enterprise-level locked-in situation to a global cloud hijack. It makes sense to not choose your cloud provider lightly.

One matter is the ease with which you may want to switch software suppliers in the future. Another concern is the true ownership and handling of the data belonging to the organization. It may provide enormous benefits in the area of efficiency to move your applications into the cloud. Companies are improving their efficiency rates of applied functionality tenfold and even a hundredfold. Reports that took weeks to produce now take minutes. Often, they do things in a cloud environment that they simply could not do before. Easy interchangeability and scaling of applications are accessible without the in-house development costs of the past. However, there should be some sort of contingency plan in place for the scenario when it becomes necessary to change a technology partner, as the consequences could be larger than what was imagined upfront.

MAKE INNOVATIVE TECHNOLOGY HUMAN
Technology has always been an extension of human existence. Some may discuss whether technology is an extension of ourselves as human beings and, hence, a part of nature itself. This requires looking at technology as a way of human expression and performing will. Others sense technology as something unnatural and fragmented in comparison with nature. This is an area of discussion worth an entire book in itself, yet one shared piece

of common ground is that people need to be able to relate technology to applicable human problems. If technology is not directly influencing the outcome of a human problem, then it is not valuable. What a human problem may consist of can vary widely, but if the public does not recognize that a specific piece of tech is resolving anything a human can relate to, then this piece of tech becomes void and cancels itself out. To put it simply, if no one understands what the new technology is good for, it will likely not be built.

Looking at any use case imaginable that has been materialized successfully, they all share the common trait that important stakeholders have understood the value it could provide. The use case triggers a valuable human understanding. It is not strictly necessary for a hugely complex use case to be understood by most people, but it sure helps when more people can understand the potential value of a use case in a short period of time. An instinctive understanding of a use case among as many stakeholders as possible makes it more attractive for development.

Finding the right use cases at the right time is a balancing act. Understanding what breaking technology is compared to what the public and market perceive it to be requires a sweet spot where attractive use cases can be built. The market will often be years and even decades behind ground-breaking technology as it evolves in test facilities around the world. Before the public can understand the human value of a use case, it is arduous to develop, launch and scale it successfully. In short, the market sentiment needs to be ready for the innovation before it can be launched and scaled successfully.

Any successful tech innovation needs to evolve in that sweet spot of human understanding. The stakeholders may vary from a few business leaders and domain experts to a wider market audience, depending on the nature of the use case. A shared understanding of the human value and the human problem that needs to be solved must be established for the use case to be realized and scaled successfully.

ANCHORING TECHNOLOGY IN ALL BUSINESS PLANS
Be aware of how your business model may shift when tech is applied efficiently. This requires the business to be proactive in dealing with technology, even when the innovation itself is not technical. Usually, tech forms part of a new product, process, or internal function to be developed. Consider a product as analog as a loaf of bread, and try to imagine how

much and in what way its value chain is digital. Most likely, no part of it will be fully analog the way it used to be. You may not need technology itself for your business to be successful, but you will need your company to be anchored in software and technology to maximize your success.

No matter how analog the product or service is, the organization providing it will be digitally dependent in some way. Ensuring that every business plan and every project includes a digital dimension may contribute to easing digitalization when the need is there.

It is often thought-provoking to observe how digitized the production lines for analog products are. The use of CAD applications and 3D printing of analog products introduces entire digital scientific environments for what are seemingly basic products. The fender of your car may be one piece of plastic, but the digital skills required to form and produce it match the competence of any rocket scientist.

By including digitalization in every business plan and project, the organization creates a digital check on its business, both internally and externally. In a perfect world, all organizations should utilize a digital portfolio management system that prevents accidental or erratic purchases of unnecessary software. A digitally seamless business execution is a dream most companies strive for but seldom or never reach. Quality checkpoints on digitalization are the minimum requirement for any organization to adjust its functions in a digital world. An analog product may be perfect, and all related digitalization may be kept to a minimum if desired. Still, a conscious approach towards a digital world involves gauging how much of the product and its value chain need to be digital.

The extreme version of this would be for a company to start off at the drawing board with a digital twin of the entire enterprise, production line, and core value chain. Sometimes the product itself will be entirely digitized too. Many companies do this today. They are born as digital sketches, facilitating control of the entire building and operational phases. The other extreme is companies that have analog products or services that are made in environments and organizations that are not digitized in any way. An artisanal loaf of bread would be a good example of an analog product. Still, there are digital sales channels, digital supply chains, and entire digital processes and value chains supporting the production, so the production environment and organization would still be digitized. Avoiding the digital part of the world is a utopia for most, so it makes sense to map it and scale it into the organization, environment, market, product, or value chains in a planned manner. In this way, the digital approach may become proactive and efficient, besides being a reaction to a need demonstrated by a digitalized world.

WIN-WIN BETWEEN BUSINESS AND TECH PRODUCTION

Often, the business side makes demands on IT, and production environments are taxing, at best, for the IT department. On the other side of the scale, there are times when the IT department and the production environment go haywire. Introducing technological changes and digitalization that are barely checked in with the business side can be problematic.

IT costs are often considered a necessary evil, and basic IT services are often outsourced, increasingly service-based, and purchased from external providers. This can be a good way to save on expenses in the area of IT. Organizations are increasingly looking at anything beyond basic IT services as an investment opportunity to support the core business in some way. IT investments supporting internal processes and internal functions will continue to be needed. The perspective of IT as a business enabler is gaining a significant foothold.

The better the IT education in the organization, the greater the chances of making tech a crucial enabler for the business side. The increasing understanding of tech in most organizations grows the understanding internally of how IT can be leveraged to create business value. The IT department and related tech development are central players in the business strategy. When IT succeeds in contributing to the value of the business, then the internal culture is also ready to capitalize on win-win situations.

Many large organizations have more than one IT department. This is often due to different requirements in different applications of technology as well as straight-out different IT solutions being sought after. More and more, basic IT is being offered by external suppliers who can provide simple, scalable, and affordable solutions to organizations. Procurement departments are progressively replacing traditional IT departments, which formerly handled basic IT services.

This means that the in-house skillsets of procurement, service management, and negotiation are slowly replacing much of the basic IT skills. In parallel, highly specialized in-house IT departments are providing the required specialist tech services needed to run core operations directly affecting the core value chains of the specific business, the core product or service production line, as well as the special internal operations.

Many IT providers and consulting firms have been a bit slow to pick up on this differentiation between the demands of shared IT services and specialized IT relating to the core product or production line. While it is easier to sell basic IT services and basic IT infrastructure in large volumes than to sell specialist IT services and skills in large volumes, many IT service providers are attempting to do both. An increasing number of small and medium-sized specialist advisory companies are benefiting from a growing global market for specialist services. In parallel, basic IT service providers often hire specialists and then risk wasting their narrow competence by placing these consultants and advisors in general IT project roles.

In traditional tech companies, there is a deeply ingrained culture of senior management requiring junior staff to do an internal 'tour of duty' for years to get to know the general support functions of IT projects. This does not benefit the people holding the specialist competence or the clients who require fresh and recent competence in cutting-edge technology in specialist areas. This means that smaller and medium-sized specialist consulting companies, as well as small and medium-sized specialist software providers, are claiming a growing market share where traditional IT providers and consulting firms are losing some of the ground they used to claim. Maintaining domain experts in-house is expensive and time-consuming. The challenge of balancing specialist and general competence is often handed to HR instead of being part of a proactive company strategy that creates a clear-cut approach to a changing market. Senior management, sometimes overly optimistic, believes they can maintain both generalist and specialist competence in-house.

Large companies providing basic IT infrastructure and IT services have been claiming their share of the IT service market for decades and are often highly specialized in outsourcing globally. The largest IT service providers may be able to maintain the various skills needed globally to serve a wide array of specialist IT service markets as well as being leading providers of basic IT.

Some examples of IT service providers are Cognizant, Infosys, and IBM. Typically, companies native to typical outsourcing destinations have become specialized in providing IT services. Primarily in a range of more universal operational IT services and infrastructure for a global market. Specialized IT services have followed close suit. Some examples are companies like Tata Consultancy Services and Wipro, which are both global reach outsourcing companies based in India and serve large global client bases. These companies are, to a large extent, specialists at outsourcing, sometimes outsourcing their own services to third countries to save even more costs for themselves and for the end customer.

For some, it does not make sense to divide IT service providers into specialists in basic IT services and specialists in specialized IT. For most clients purchasing outsourced services, it will make sense to understand which IT service provider they specifically should go to for outsourcing. They need to know whether such a partnership will provide seamless, low-cost shared IT services and if specialized advisors are required as part of the package. It is significant to comprehend the difference between aiming for seamless shared services provided from a different country, continent, and culture and being in need of business-driven technology services.

There is a current awakening taking place in the IT markets globally where the nuances of business-driven tech investments and general IT services that are generally easier to provide at a low cost are becoming clearer. There may still be a zillion reasons for top management to choose one IT service provider over another, but the diversion of domain-driven market segments is becoming clearer. This development is aligned with technology investments that are business-driven and those that are not.

DATA AND MARKET DOMAINS MOVING INTO THE FUTURE

The current large cloud data platform providers are currently shifting the application of technology into the future, and they are moving fast. For many, it remains to be seen what the future will look like when it comes to making a choice between the providers and the various variations of solution offerings. The question intensifies whether companies want to move into the cloud with their core processes and data after all. There are some trends crystallizing into a future map towards the cloud for various market segments and verticals. Microsoft, Google, Amazon, and Apple together form a new form of western hemisphere hegemony in data platforms handling data processing in the cloud. Meta, Alibaba, and Huawei are other examples of large corporations putting their stakes in a fast-growing cloud race. Meta is contributing with user mass and social capital, while Alibaba and Huawei are examples of Chinese counterparts to the various American corporate examples.

As Meta, through Facebook, has claimed its share of our social life in the cloud, there are others either scrambling or emerging to find their place in the tech sky. It can be a confusing landscape to navigate. Currently, it looks like Microsoft, Amazon, and Google are coming to grips with emerging markets and possibilities for innovation and expansion. They build on the years of experience end-users have accumulated with their initial utilization of cloud data platforms. While Amazon has clearly claimed its market space in retail, Microsoft has claimed its space in the corporate world by chasing operational processes and administrative functions. For Microsoft, this is a natural expansion from the office terminal operating system that conquered the world in the 1990s. Currently, the focus for Microsoft, Amazon, and Google is on gaining ownership of domain-specific value chains. From the outside, it can look like these three actors are dividing much of the western world among themselves.

The introduction of digital currencies like Bitcoin and the Chinese Digital Yuan has created a bit of havoc in the financial world. The Chinese Digital Yuan was the first major central bank digital currency (CBDC) to be rolled out. The Chinese government started the exploration of a national digital currency in 2014, and it was officially launched in close concurrency with the Chinese winter Olympics in 2022. Trust in financial transactions can now be leveraged not only by the largest global tech companies but also by newly established digital stock exchanges, or crypto exchanges. Trust in the currency markets is partly shifting from traditional banks to tech companies. At the moment, it looks like markets are gaining trust in cryptocurrencies, while most national banks are scrambling to find ways through regulation to retain the trust they have owned for millennia as issuers of currencies.

When I was writing this book, the largest contenders claiming financial value chains were the ones owning the largest and most commonly used data platforms globally. In the western world, they are Microsoft, Amazon, Google, and perhaps Apple. These are current contenders to take on the battle for a large part of the trust mantle that banks are forced to share in one way or another. These large companies are the actors in the western world that currently possess enough data about the end-users to control their behavior. They own the end-user interfaces required and can form complete financial value chains. It may not be far-fetched to see that by controlling financial end-user behavior, a few tech giants alone own the capacity to steer core capital value streams in the direction they choose.

Let's look at the example of Amazon and books. Amazon has expanded its retail value chain and controls the user journey from potentially published authors to the e-book downloaded on Kindle. In this process, money will potentially change hands between the author, the publisher, and the end-user purchasing the book. We have already discussed how the retailer is omitted for the benefit of Amazon and seemingly for the convenience of the end-user. Part of keeping up digitally for smaller online retailers has been to connect to credit card companies' user interfaces, PayPal services, and other payment solutions in their online shops. Until recently, they handed the payment channels over to financial institutions and an emerging myriad of fintech wallet solutions.

The question that emerges is if an end customer would like to purchase a Kindle book online using a digital currency, **what stands in the way for Amazon to take partial or complete ownership of a digital currency as well as the financial value stream?** Including the moment of the transaction? There will be no direct need for any bank to be involved in that value stream at all anymore. This is far from being about obsolete payment options on the online platform. This is about who owns the issuance of the currency itself and the chain of payments made with it. This power is now being handed to global tech companies and their associates while regulators certainly are not ahead of the game.

This is a good moment to remember that the world does not even know who the real issuer of Bitcoin is. The name Satoshi Nakamoto is referred to as the inventor of bitcoin, but in fact, this is a pseudonym. Googling the origins and issuing ownership of Bitcoin will not reveal who is behind this global cryptocurrency. El Salvador was the first country in the world to make Bitcoin an official currency by law on June 9, 2021. When an entire country puts such trust in a privately issued cryptocurrency of unknown origin, what are the implications when a nation like China introduces its own cryptocurrency and has the capacity to enforce its use?

In the case of Bitcoin, there is little, if any, publicly known transparency or control over its capital streams. The tools to do so are not commonly shared beyond young and private crypto exchanges, and the skill sets required and understanding of the situation are not yet sufficiently established among lawmakers and national bureaucracies.

When, and perhaps no longer if, digital currencies will be used by a large number of people in place of state-owned analog currencies, they hold the potential to cause major disruption in the current banking and monetary systems. In the case of the Chinese Digital Yuan, it will be the Chinese state that will own the digital capital flows of individual spenders. This will place the Chinese government in a position to influence the capital streams according to their own wishes and ideals. This can be done by rewarding certain spending behaviors or outright making unwanted transactions unavailable for named individuals. A state that owns its own digital currency as well as the digital capital flows of its spending will be able to steer the digital capital value streams entirely.

It is worth noticing that while China is a forerunner in the introduction of digital currency, many national banks of other countries are struggling to keep up their preparations for a national digital currency. The Bahamas introduced a national digital currency in 2020, and since then, Nigeria and Jamaica have followed suit. According to ABC News in 2023, more than 20 other countries are currently running trial projects, while, for instance, the UK is not ready to introduce a national digital currency until at least some time during the second half of the 2020s.

Just like the telecom markets got disrupted as mobile phone technology skipped the need for landline phone infrastructure, digital currencies are now disrupting the need for banks. The global race to set up mobile cell towers in developing countries where landline infrastructure was not in place has enabled a lot of areas to skip landline infrastructure entirely since the 1990s. Hence, the first phone many people in developing countries owned became a mobile device, or even a smartphone. In the same way, national digital currencies are now enabling people who don't have bank accounts to gain access to financial systems and bypass banks entirely by using digital currencies on their smartphones. There are few places in the world where this financial disruption has been more instrumental to societal development than in Africa south of the Sahara. Small-scale business investments are becoming possible for millions of people who did not have access to bank services ten years ago. This enabler, together with new and large capital streams of investments from Asia in particular, is changing the face of the world, and it's happening fast. I would encourage any reader who is curious about this to find a source of information she or he trusts and look up the GDP for countries globally. The economic shift of value creation and value distribution globally during the last two decades is astounding and is likely to put much of the bad news that unfortunately still sells better in the shadows. At the same time, the situation is truly a nightmare for global and national financial regulatory bodies, which may not have been particularly forward-leaning and tech-savvy to start with. There is a current gold rush going on for data, consumers, and business adventures outside the traditional power nations, which bypasses established structures and institutions on a large scale. Even if the lawlessness of such disruption may be real, it is also great news for any nation, society, village, or individual that could not participate in economic growth due to a lack of access to financial infrastructure until recently.

According to Investopedia, some governments are coming up with attempts to control and register transactions made with Bitcoin. Many financial and government institutions, particularly among traditionally powerful nations, are still warning about the risks of cryptocurrencies. Investor alerts have been issued by US institutions: the Securities and Exchange Commission[35] (SEC), the Financial Industry Regulatory Authority[36] (FINRA), the Consumer Financial Protection Bureau[37] (CFPB), and other agencies.

I am afraid the battles over owning capital streams and digital currencies are getting closer to being lost by traditional financial institutions and governments alike. For every step tech companies are taking forward, they increasingly claim control of capital value streams and, recently, in some cases, the currency as well. Authoritative nations may clamp down hard on independent cryptocurrencies through regulation to maintain the issuing authority of currencies and control of chosen value chains in the markets. More liberal countries may try to find a middle way through regulation and the introduction of their own national digital currencies, competing with independent ones. The challenge of independent cryptocurrencies being global may force some nations to resist them and close off parts of the international crypto trade. As most nations are now latecomers to the world of digital currencies, national banks may see themselves beaten by global fintech currency actors, leaving them seemingly few options other than prohibition to retain the power and trust of local currency. This may not work very well, as we have seen cryptocurrencies increasingly gain trust and become a more naturalized part of global financial mechanisms. It is now clear that, for example, Bitcoin and other widely distributed cryptocurrencies, though still fairly volatile, respond to market events just as naturally as other currencies, minerals, shares, securities, and other investment objects. Regulation is therefore on its way in many places,

---

35   https://www.investopedia.com/terms/s/sec.asp
36   https://www.investopedia.com/terms/f/finra.asp
37   https://www.investopedia.com/terms/c/consumer-financial-protection-bureau-cfpb.asp

even if some regulators are a bit late to the party. It is also a challenge that the traditional regulatory bodies are not built for digital regulation, which means that digital regulation often becomes distributed across various agencies. Crypto exchanges, including decentralized exchanges, are expanding their global financial importance fast, while regulators are trying to find new ways to enforce fresh laws in unfamiliar terrain. Hacking and money laundering now form a universal challenge as banks, nations, and most digital citizens struggle to find new ways to deal with new problems.

We have not seen the end game of crypto yet, but this is an ongoing global race for ownership of currencies and value streams. This race is as great as any other tech revolution in our history. In parallel, it can be pointedly seen as a 'mere race for data,' resulting in insight and control. We are increasingly getting used to cash-free value chains where all transactions are digital. As we are increasingly digitizing our environment, we are putting our individual powers into the hands of others—often generated on different continents than where we may reside—so we have little to say about how that power is used.

In many ways, the issuing of digital currencies offers new ways for tech companies to tell the world that they are inventing their own digital money presses and bringing their own digital currencies to consumers and investors globally. The moment mass usage of digital currencies becomes the norm, tech companies will own the trust in the currency and the digital transaction, and in many ways, we are getting there. It has been said that tech companies are becoming larger and more powerful than many sovereign states. It seems they understand the potential of monetary power in the cybersphere and are rigging themselves to increasingly apply that power globally.

The World Bank is stating that 20 of the world's largest economies are establishing official standards for regulating and issuing sovereign digital currencies by 2025[38]. The race for national banks across the world to enable the use of digital currencies is a tactical necessity as the competition between national-issued currencies and privately issued digital currencies is on. The Facebook digital currency Diem[39], formerly known as Libra, is an example of how one of the largest global tech companies has tried to

---

38 https://www.coindesk.com/imf-world-bank-g7-countries-to-create-central-bank-digital-currency-rules
39 https://en.wikipedia.org/wiki/Diem_(digital_currency)#European_Union_regulatory_response

issue its own sovereign currency. Based on a universal user hegemony in their vertical, social networks, and the following global trust in their online platform. If it had been successful, Libra would have had Facebook as its central bank. In 2020, the e-commerce site Shopify entered the Libra Association, so, in theory, we could start to see the contours of a longer capital value stream between the two tech companies entering the fintech scene. In real life, Libra has faltered for several reasons, mostly due to a lack of trust from existing financial institutions and governments alike. Libra has also experienced online safety issues of various kinds, including information privacy concerns.

In the conglomerate of evolving e-wallets, online payment solutions, cryptocurrencies, crypto exchanges, and digital currencies, traditional banks, international finance institutions, national governments, and global tech corporations are currently engaging in a huge race to secure trust in their payment methods and processes—trust that equals entitlement to digitized money and its digital pathways.

I may exaggerate, but I would like to point out how 'anyone' who is rich and tech-savvy enough can now invent their own digital currency press and lay out custom-made monetary pathways across the internet. States, financial institutions, banks, and corporate tech companies are not necessarily so different anymore, and it seems the tech companies are leaping ahead to claim their market share in the capital value stream race.

When it comes to government stakeholders, the World Bank has definite plans to mitigate and control the situation, while the Chinese state is clearly leading the race at scale when it comes to national digital currency. The Chinese control of the capital value streams can be done by controlling the transactional moment. Banks may desire to keep their monopoly of the transactional moment while ensuring state control and insight into traditional digital transactional systems.

It is not certain that the state-owned sovereign currencies will prevail in the future in the same way they have until now. The world is enduring a seismic monetary shift enabled by the fintech industry and global tech enterprises. In the near future, there will be more new digital monetary tech solutions and new capital value streams emerging with new tech owners. Data collection will form a huge part of this new mosaic of payment streams controlled by tech giants.

Right now, there is a gold rush for data gathering in agriculture. A few years ago, water distribution and usage in the field were initially entered into the cloud. GPS technology was applied to optimize the use of water for elevating crop yields in arid areas. The harvesting machines themselves are now collecting huge amounts of data, using sensor technology to detect space between plants and re-applying numerous datasets with algorithms to optimize the positioning and number of seeds being planted. Satellites are collecting visual, weather, and geological datasets from space, which are again contextualized with data collections in real-time on the ground.

Only a few years ago, visual inspections formed the basis for decision-making in the field. The farmer would look at a few plants and make judgements on when and how to harvest. Today, autonomous robots move around the fields measuring the ripeness, size and position of a far larger part of the produce. Algorithms are applied to produce precise estimates for when the harvest should happen. This new value chain of data in the field can yet be combined with other value chains like power consumption in greenhouses, logistic supply chains for post-harvest packaging and transport of produce to the end customers. There is really no end to how digital value chains can be built and interconnected. Starting with domain expert systems tapping into other domain expert systems resulting in ever larger and more complex value chains.

As the climate changes in larger parts of the world, scarcity of water will drive the tech evolution of water management beyond what we can imagine today. And it will happen fast.

THE INSIGHT-DRIVEN MARKET FOR DATA PLATFORMS
In the last decade, the startup scene has overflowed with cloud data platforms, bringing insight in various ways. It took me some time to realize what many tech innovations—labeled products, software, IaaS, PaaS, and SaaS—actually do. These often analyze and present data in new ways, providing new insights. However, there are some other data platform products that do something new beyond being a strong new analytical tool for data. By adding insight directly to or into products, digital product management becomes an entirely new ballgame.

The first time I started using Microsoft Azure and contextualizing datasets by myself was in 2015. I was surprised at how easy it was to set up business intelligence dashboards, constructing all kinds of insights from the Excel files and live stream data I had at hand. It only took me a few hours to get the hang of how to do it. If I had been 20 years younger, it probably would have taken even less time. There is no real programming involved. By using a developer's studio interface, I could easily upload data and make the most amazing visual comparisons of information. I was impressed by this first taste of the new low-entry level of performing data contextualization. Data analytics was made accessible beyond the realm of hard-core programmers.

This, and other similar easy access to data systems and the contextualization of it, have enabled a high number of startups to build apps that easily solve one or two problems for end-users. Advanced data contextualization providers are building solutions containing a higher number of data types. Imagine an industrial app showing you a 3D model of a gas pump where you can see everything from the live operational information of input flow, output flow, power consumption, and GPS position all in an operational landscape. In the 3D model, you can also see ERP-based datasets describing which parts of the pump were maintained, inspected, and installed by whom. In this example, we are already layering five live data types and three historical ERP data types. In addition to the 3D model itself, which is a static picture in this case. In other cases, it could be a live video stream from the operational site.

It took me some time working with these kinds of insight platforms before it dawned on me that all I was working with was insight. There was no information feedback loop providing reprocessed information back into the platform. The reason being that the moment data processing is involved and processed data goes back into the solution—for instance, through decision-making engines—the solution becomes far more complex and is likely to lose much of its flexibility.

The mindset in many industries around the world has been formed by a generation of ERP users. Many middle-aged process engineers expect a UX to provide an option for them to provide manual input. The mind shift of sensors automating all input and using highly complex solutions for insight only dazzles some who have worked in analog industries for decades. The general understanding of value creation from mere insight is growing across industries globally. The human input factor is slowing down complex solutions, and expertise is used more efficiently by observing rather than by crunching numbers.

MOVING FROM PROCESS CONTROL TO INSIGHT

One enormous shift in mindset taking place, parallel with big data expanding and interconnecting the world around us, is how digital systems and domain expert tools are decreasingly being made to maintain control at every link in the value chain. This is not to say that control is not important anymore. This is to say that industries are moving beyond what they used to control while hooking up new and larger digital systems to their initial control solutions. Product quality and production output used to be achieved by taking control of specific core production processes. In recent years, an increasing number of new digital solutions have taken control for granted as more data and information are available than ever before. The shift taking place now is that an increasing amount of insight into an existing process is used to make bottleneck decisions where needed. It may not be the most important thing to keep control of every minuscule part of the core value chain, but it is vital to have insight and understanding of pivotal moments in the core production process and to steer that very point towards optimization.

To put this shift in perspective, one may compare a greenhouse with tomatoes to an Olympic athlete. For so long, humanity has been concerned with the caretaking, training, and work going into the process before the prime moment when the tomatoes are harvested or the very day the athlete enters the main competition—the *performing* result matter. The focus has been on the process of building components, growth, and the best possible care prior to reaching peak performance. The tomatoes need to be large, evenly shaped, bright red, and ripe at the perfect point to gain the best-selling price. The athlete needs to be in the best possible physical shape by the date the Olympic competition takes place. This is universally the only and best way to achieve the desired results; there is no questioning that.

As all steps are made for optimal output, the world moves from a focus on process towards insight. Process focus expands and transcends into results. The fourth industrial revolution keeps an eye out for bottlenecks in the production line and shifts the general vantage point from control to prediction. Control is already established, so the question is what is beyond control. Increased insight into new datasets brings possibilities for a changed mode of operation. Doing what has been considered the 'right thing' is falling out of fashion as new technology is enabling disruptive ways of reaching the same goal in a simpler way, providing better results.

Overly complicated processes are overdue to be replaced by simpler and smarter solutions.

For centuries, even millennia, librarians have meticulously developed and applied cataloging systems. The systems have varied to some extent between cultures. Best practices and simple principles of following numbers and letters have been considered universal. Systems have evolved and dwindled, yet the basic principles have been considered universal.

Then, someone got the idea to use a drone equipped with a video camera to fly by all library shelves every night, recording every bar code, title, and author of every book where it had been placed by its latest user. For millennia, librarians have spent a substantial amount of their time putting so-called misplaced books back in the right position according to letters and numbers. Now, by looking into the library data system every morning, the librarian can see exactly where each book is placed by the visiting public. In a stroke of digital innovation, the entire science of cataloging is not exactly eradicated, but at least seriously disrupted.

Next, try to imagine how books are placed within this new system compared to earlier. I find it amusing to think of how this drone indexing solution was tried out in children's libraries in its early phases before it got introduced, for instance, into academia. In place of following a rule-based system that was created to imitate fields of thoughts contained in books, the system is now following the intuition of the end-user and the natural placement system of our human brain (a brain that could be in an absent-minded mode). Librarians need not spend energy placing books back into a static system that needs to be learned. The system has evolved to observe, understand, and replicate how we humans do something in a natural way in the first place.

This change disrupts the system, making it shift from a forced, controlling behavior to insight-based bottleneck decisions. I could imagine that the most boring books for kids would easily be stuck in the midst of some shelves placed far from the library entry and reading spaces. In my mind, I can picture how the most popular cartoons may be left on low shelves close to the door as parents remove them from their kids' hands as one of the last things they do before leaving the library. My anticipation may not be correct, but I would suspect there is far less randomness to such random book placements than what we would have guessed a decade ago. What has been considered chaos is simply natural human behavior where recognizable patterns exist

To me, this example describes how we have been overly busy trying to implement control systems and structures in places where insight has been lacking. Instead of trying to control the world around us, future generations may be on the verge of letting go of at least some rigid structures and leaning into what has been considered more random and chaotic.

I am aware that this shift from perceived control of the process to result-oriented insight is far from a black-and-white affair. There are some large conundrums in this picture that are worth keeping in check. First, in most cases, there is someone or something that benefits from keeping the process under tight control. Nobody is letting go of control easily, as there is always someone else eager to take over the reins. Disrupting systems shift control of power to new hands, while control will always be held by someone in some way. In many of the cases described in this book, large global tech companies are the ones taking control of the new value chains and benefiting from the global shifts taking place. Where control used to be the powerhouse, insight is opening a new realm as to what control really is and how it can be enacted.

THE FUTURE OF DOMAIN EXPERTISE

Let there be no doubt: domain expertise will be needed for the application of AI in the future. Machines will, in general, not be able to replace human knowledge and insight. It is our human insight that is being reflected in AI and big data solutions, and there will always be a need for domain experts to hold the expertise entered into such systems. Without human skills being implemented in AI models, there will be no sensible output coming from solutions involving AI.

That said, there may be fewer domain experts needed in the future. As expertise is replicable and scalable in systems, fewer domain experts are required. This brings forward the question of what domain expertise will look like in the future, as fewer experts may be educated in each field and fewer may be practicing actively within their fields. By removing domain expertise from the production floor and increasingly entering skills into centrally operated systems, the number of skilled heads in each domain will decrease over time. There is a possibility that a global reduction in expert personnel costs over time could erode the overall richness of knowledge.

For the sake of the thought experiment, I compare various fields of human expertise with biodiversity in nature. An increasing number of biodiverse landscapes are being replaced with homogeneous agricultural landscapes. Humanity has long paid attention to the increased yields of produce. As the vulnerabilities of homogeneous crops are gradually discovered, measures are taken to combat diseases, fungi, and other emerging threats to the crops resulting from large-scale homogeneous farming. The increased focus on climate change, pollution, and the plain removal of biotopes following the replacement of biodiverse natural habitats by homogeneous agriculture opens up a well of conflicting views. Human building mass, urban sprawl, and an exodus into the countryside to get away from cityscapes are claiming nature at an exponential pace. Entire shifts in belief systems lead to endless discussions about what is happening.

So many chains of reason have been built upon financial, environmental, emotional, national, egoistic, political, and holistic values. It has become nothing less than dizzying for an individual to capture the essence of what is going on. Academia keeps producing research while adding detail to the obvious, which is not always welcomed by all or received in a constructive context. So many opinions are being presented as exclusive and exhaustive truths, and sadly, the truth is often opposed and framed as a subjective opinion.

I run the risk of holding a partial vantage point myself; however, I am convinced that the core of the challenge is that diversity in itself is replaced. This is as close as I can get to a universal observation on the topic. That means I can compare the overall narrative of removing diversity in the area of domain expertise. When that happens, domain expertise will come under pressure from a lack of richness, diversity, and naturally occurring organic continuity. When knowledge becomes globally unified, large, and simplified for all, our future evolution of insight will be threatened as aggregated complexity, richness, and the number of varied details will be reduced. This is a principle that applies to technology as much as it applies to nature or humanity. If we simplify any large and diverse entity to make it more efficient, homogeneous, and accessible for all, then we will end up paying the price of losing diversity, continuous organic growth, and self-sustainable systems.

In parallel, there is always hope that new fields of expertise will emerge in the spaces left after outdated domains have ceased to exist. Nature has a wonderful way to recover and grow new landscapes, given that there is space left for emergence.

I fear that large-scale placement of human capital in the form of systematized and centralized new technology can create human friction, polarization, and confusion. Does anyone remember Margaret Thatcher closing coal mines in England in the 1980s? When jobs expire and people are told that their skills are no longer required, upheaval is likely. Every shift in paradigm throughout history has left some behind, and often the ones left behind have not been the ones to tell the story. Not until a new normal has been reached by most, with new jobs requiring new skills, will a new stable era in the industry be reached. This time it is not manual labor that becomes obsolete; it is professionals in domains like engineering, customer service, sales, accounting, drivers, design, inventory, logistics, controllers, banking, publishing, marketing, and many other areas that need to adjust to a new 'smart' realm.

At this point, I run the risk of introducing philosophical rabbit holes inspired by George Orwell's *1984*. I am exploring observations on innovation, technology, and change, and I like to observe principles at least as much as narratives. There is a universal pendulum moving in the space between complexity and simplicity. Imagine that human capital of diverse experience will be quenched by large fields of applied technology, and human insights will then be stifled in a systemic tech grid. Then the pendulum will swing back at some point, as such a system will starve the very source of insight it relies on to provide value and propel forward.

Some may notice that in my reasoning, I have also provided an easy way out for our shared global environmental problems. My intention could not be further from the truth. Simplifying such a complex constellation of perhaps the largest problem humanity has experienced is not my intention. My goal is to describe a natural process over a long period where growing complexities naturally get exchanged for simplicity before complexity continues to grow in yet another cycle. Eventually, the complexity would become so great that it could not hold its weight anymore. It may subside or collapse and give space for a new development towards complexity. From my vantage point, this process is similar in any field. Various forms of diversity surrounding us will, over time, be replaced by something more homogeneous that will again evolve into more complexity by yielding to its own weaknesses. It will break up or evolve. The pendulum of change will keep moving between what is possible and what is not, in terms of complexity and diversity.

When innovating, developing human insight will always require stretching. Domain experts will benefit from and often deepen their understanding of their own domain when technology is applied in a new way in their field. Innovation can pull evolving domain insight forward with every successful application of a newly developed use case. This mutual pull and push between domain expertise and the introduction of technology may very well be a smaller-scale model. However, evolving complexity will propel a domain and adhering to innovative solutions forward into an increasingly paced evolution process. This will go on as long as there are resources available to keep growing insight and domain expertise.

THE FIELD OF INNOVATION
At this point, it feels natural to take a step back and take a look at the field of innovation. What is it, and how can we all best use it? Science, in general, has a lot to say about this. Many corporate research departments claim to be part of the global innovation field. I find many of the frameworks I have worked with somehow limiting. They are often dividing innovation into domains and fields instead of working from a principle-based vantage point. I believe innovation as a principle-based concept holds more importance than innovation described in product, market, human development, or any other defined area. I prefer to experience innovation as an inside-out event and not as an observation of what is possible in a limited space.

Some use systems similar to recipes or step stones towards innovation and find these techniques useful[40]. Among others, Hekkert has written scientifically about technological innovation systems[41] and the required dynamics and functions for innovation to be successful. Hekkert has not been a direct inspiration for my work. His concepts provide a good example of how one can enhance the results and quality of innovation by observing the dynamics of an organization and applying principles and navigation tools throughout the process.

In recent years, there has been a strong shift towards sustainable innovation. No matter how valid the introduction of sustainability in

40   M.P. Hekkert, R.A.A. Suurs, S.O. Negro, S. Kuhlmann, R.E.H.M. Smits, *Functions of Innovation Systems: A New Approach for Analyzing Technological Change, Technological Forecasting & Social Change* 74 (2007) 413-432.
41   https://en.wikipedia.org/wiki/Technological_innovation_system#Seven_system_functions

innovation is, we are once again defining a space that makes innovation in a confined area more accessible. By introducing checks and balances on sustainability, we add process to the fundamentally open space of innovation. While a shared taxonomy on sustainability is a good thing, the risk exists that innovative thought is hampered by pre-defined sets of requirements. Sustainable innovation experiences hyperbolic growth globally. An emerging economy can arise when financial benefits and branding are cultivated for the sake of universal wellbeing. Sustainability is a great invention in itself, yet moral branding may not benefit freedom of thought in the long run. Sustainability could be a step on the way to something else. In other words, who knows what sustainability may lead to or provide for in a hundred years? It could be something grand, or at least different from what it looks like now.

I do return to the pendulum, moving between the points of what is possible between simplicity and complexity. The space where human understanding of value resulting from innovation takes place is a requirement for the creative process to happen. Reading about Galileo Galilei was my first time learning about someone thinking innovatively. He was looking at known objects (celestial objects) from a new vantage point, while he was considered wrong in every way by the authorities of his time. Galileo may be best known for his astronomical discoveries; his most famous was that the Earth indeed circles the sun and not the other way around. The sun circling Earth was considered a universal truth until he spoke differently. In the process of making these discoveries, he invented various tools to demonstrate and document his observations. His most famous invention was the telescope.

My intention in bringing up Galileo, remembered as an astronomer, is that he had the idea that the universe worked differently than what most imagined. Then he invented technology to demonstrate and prove his ideas. I like to think that Galileo was a great innovator who is historically decorated by the notion that he refined the method for developing tech use cases of his time. The fact that he was persecuted by an inquisition of the Catholic Church for his ideas proves to me that his ideas and innovations were clearly outside the maturity level of his peers. It took courage and persistence to move beyond that space of limited human understanding of what he wanted to create and elucidate in his lifetime.

I do believe innovators in many organizations experience at least some of the same resistance today. Especially when trying to convey to leadership

DIGITIZED PRODUCT MANAGEMENT

the value of a given invention that will cost money and resources to develop. Again, we are back to that space of opportunity existing between what has already been developed and manifested in the real world and what is possible, acceptable, and functional for a large enough part of the audience in the near future. If Galileo lived today, I would like to imagine that he would still be happy to apply some principle-based methods to develop his tech innovations and use cases.

CONCLUSION

Once again, I find myself in a meeting with senior vice presidents of a large industrial conglomerate. This time, I want to open up the conversation about the potential value of use cases across their internal operations. The most tech-savvy VP of the company proudly shares with the rest of us how the division has purchased two robots that are used for inspection of heavy machinery on some selected industrial installations. It is a pilot project, but the results are promising. Beyond improving HSSQ challenges by removing workers from operational environments and allowing them to work from the safety and comfort of the control room, it will be a cost-reducing venture. Applying wandering robots reduces the time spent on manual inspections by 20%. I believe all in the room, including myself, are impressed and a bit awed by the videos of dog-like machines walking around the production floor. They look like dogs; they can walk stairs like dogs; they can see perhaps more than dogs; hear better than dogs; and even have a sense of smell like dogs.

At this very moment, tech is fun, exciting, and visionary. Everybody in the room is fascinated by what the robot can *do*. I refrain from excusing myself as I carefully start to dismantle the image of this super-exciting robot taking over what has been a human function for centuries. I try to be sensitive by underlining what this robot *provides* instead of raving about what it *does*. In my worldview, it provides a lot of data. I want to leave the frenzy of how cool the robot dog is and how much fun it is to operate it. I want to talk about the data it delivers.

To start with, data may seem far more boring than a fun, interactive, playful machine dog. I am sure it could bark if I wanted it to. Yet the fascination of the possible use cases I throw out as I speak sparks another layer of enthusiasm. "Count the age, make, fixture, and replacement of your 14,000,000 bolts in your offshore installation and plan for optimized maintenance and replacements." This may sound hugely boring to most outside that room, but as I mention these specific benefits, many catch on to the enormous cost savings made possible in this way. Yet, the best thing is that nobody actually has to walk outside in the cold and take a look. And then, if this inspection can be done for fixtures, then what about pipes, pumps, machines, fans, vents, stairs, meters, and anything else in the production site? The level of thinking going on in the room is crushing a virtual glass ceiling, so I can imagine hearing the crash as the enthusiasm rises to new levels. Within five minutes, the idea of adding airborne and water-submersible drones is added to the picture.

Within fifteen minutes, the idea of observing the entire plant as one entity starts to materialize. We are no longer talking about inspecting that one pipe or checking the pressure on that one valve. We are talking about how to create a model that can optimize all pain points and production processes at once. In place of manually prioritizing between 276 prioritized pain points in the building mass, we will soon be able to optimize the production plant as one. We will steer this optimization based on clear parameters and values that we agree on. Efficiency, output, quality of product, and cost savings are crucial parameters we can now navigate universally because we will have benchmarks and understand what and how much value we can expect to create as a result of given measures. In short, we are lifting our view from the tech available to the data available and the opportunities provided.

As time is up and people start leaving the room, the most tech-savvy VP in the company walks up to me and exclaims, "I never thought about tech before as a mere provider of insight. This is brilliant, as it gives us the opportunity to work with HSSQ and reduce costs globally. Our workers will be so glad to hear this. Now we can focus more on the safety and efficiency of what they do instead of just adding more tech. While our tech stack is reaching the ceiling, we have been partially blind to the opportunities we already have in our existing digital tools. It is not about adding one more machine to the stack. It is about adding one more layer of data and then harvesting an exponential value potentially added by new datasets on top of what we already have!"

This is the type of meeting that I simply love. When a shared understanding of value emerges, no matter how value is perceived or measured, it opens up the understanding that there are more gems around the next corner. One small new thing adding to what we already have is creating exponential new value. This is where we are today. While hindsight has always held the corner on offering wisdom (too late), new data and complex, innovative ways to use it create an opportunity for foresight to also be 20/20. It is not for me to decide what value means for anyone else, but I can point others in the direction where they need to go to find what matters to them and give them the tools to develop their foresight. My hope is that this book can help each reader identify, find, and materialize what matters so that each unique and desired value can come true.

THE AUTHOR

As the author of *Digitized Product Management,* I offer guidance and a clear methodology for leaders, product managers, and consultants to navigate professionally through the expanding landscape referred to as Industry v4.0.

As a practicing Integral Master Coach™, I optimize extensive tools, empower human change, and teach applicable skills much needed to navigate the changing digital landscape. Therefore, high-level coaching methods weave through every aspect of my work.

For those who wish to study the impact of digitalization, *Digitized Product Management* draws parallels to natural evolution and human change principles in the same breath as making emerging technologies and their disrupting business models available to a wide audience. The vantage point on tech as an Integral Master Coach™ enables human perspective-taking on the tech-driven change happening globally today.

Global companies today must understand and balance stable and secure operations while exploring innovative connections between business and technology. My personal passion for business case building and value stream mapping is my motivation for following emerging technologies.

My mission is to provide a purposeful point of view on what is happening all around us today in the space of digitalization through innovation. The ground rules of innovation are constant principles. These rules are still applicable when artificial intelligence and agile approaches seemingly disrupt the rules of the game. My passion is to explore the dilemmas my readers face so they can better own the changes by becoming directors as opposed to reacting to the evolution of technology. My goal is to make these insights accessible, meaningful, and human.

- Agathe Daae-Qvale

THANKS

TO THIS TRIBE FOR BRINGING DREAMS INTO THE WORLD.

I would like to thank so many wonderful people who have supported me, each in their own unique way, on my journey to make this book a reality.

While editing the drafts, I just loved the learning process of writing better English. Rusti LeHay, you are a true master of words. Christer Johnsen, the persistence you have shown in seeing me through the publishing journey has been formidable. Not for a moment did you cease believing in my ability to get the word out, and for this I am truly grateful. Tobias Studer Andersson, your support and faith in this book project have been a supportive pillar for the quality of the end product. Your tangible feedback sessions helped me improve the quality of the content of this book substantially. Dalip Dewan, your gentle understanding and support for my journey have been continuous and fruitful. I believe every conversation we have had on the topics throughout this book has brought me not only delight but also closer to my professional destination. Agata Bélanger, thank you for being the first proofreader of my final draft. The way you took on the challenge and proofread so many references quickly and easily meant a lot to me. You have shown faith in both the product and in me. Rob Baak: You're a force for good, and you know it! Thank you for helping me detangle so many of the Gordian knots of professional consulting along the way. I believe you deserve a huge stage where many more can hear and learn from the depth and complexity of your consulting experiences. Thank you to my sister Camilla Daae-Qvale, who, in spite of my insistence on staying in to get my work done repeatedly, has moved me out of my usual path to enjoy art, theater, architecture, butterflies, and views so that I could find the inspiration to write what I had to say in a human way. Thank you, Holly Woods, for sharing your soul work with me and leading me to the place I had to go as a person to achieve what I needed to for myself. With or without this book on my own behalf, I truly believe every book in the world would be better with your magic dust spread over it. Thank you, Teena Clipston, for your patient and beautiful work in typesetting and for always staying in the zone of true grace, no matter my lack of grace when my life got on edge. Lieven Dubois, thank you for introducing me to the marvels of artificial intelligence in the tech world and teaching me to observe closely. What a journey it has been and still is, 30 years later. Per-Olav Opdahl, thank you for updating me on the nuts and bolts of the myriad of options this tech world continuously provides. That little hint or funny remark towards the exact bow tie, putting it all together in a new way, works wonders again and again. Asad Riaz, thank you for opening my eyes to how business really works. Since you shared some golden nuggets on business modeling with me, I can barely walk past a shop without being curious about how it is all put together, often a bit differently than what the eye first observes. Thank you, Torgeir Paulsen, for sharing your living curiosity about every technical detail in everything we see, near and far. You taught me to read in a new way, not only for pleasure but to satisfy a flowing curiosity about how anything and everything works. Thank you, Therese Vidhammer, for demonstrating with your own being for more than 50 years that if there is no heart in it, then there really is not much to go by. Thank you, Fiona Fulton and Nicola Rai, for being such amazing sounding boards. No matter how aloof or goofy the idea, you both choose to resonate with it and play with it instead of tempering it. Finally, a big thank you to my three godchildren, Malene, Alf, and Olav, for instilling hope and truth the way only children can and for sharing exactly that with everyone around.

https://tinkerblue.com/

GLOSSARY

Observing that the content of this book may be made more comprehensible for many readers by including a glossary, I decided to give ChatGPT v4 a chance to shine. I chose the input question, "Make a glossary for a digital product manager for this text...". The glossary below is what ChatGPT provided:

3D Digital Twin: A virtual representation of a physical object or system, typically created using 3D modeling techniques and enriched with data to provide a detailed and interactive digital replica.

Agile: A project management approach that emphasizes flexibility, adaptability, and iterative development.

AI models: Algorithms and systems that use artificial intelligence techniques to analyze data, learn patterns, and make predictions or decisions.

AI Use Cases: Specific scenarios or situations in which artificial intelligence (AI) technology can be applied to provide value, solve problems, or improve user experiences within a digital product.

AI: Abbreviation for Artificial Intelligence, which refers to the development of computer systems capable of performing tasks that normally require human intelligence.

Belief systems: Sets of principles, values, and ideologies that individuals or groups adhere to.

Benchmark: A reference point or standard used for comparison and evaluation, often representing the best-known performance or quality in a particular context.

Best practices: Established methods, techniques, or processes that are widely recognized as effective or efficient in a particular domain.

Big data: Extremely large and complex data sets that cannot be easily managed, processed, or analyzed using traditional data processing techniques.

Big Hairy Audacious Goals (BHAG): Ambitious and challenging goals set by organizations to achieve significant changes or transformations.

Business model: The plan or strategy that outlines how a company creates, delivers, and captures value from its products or services.

Capital Streams: The flow of financial resources, such as investments, transactions, and funds, within a financial system.

CEO: Chief Executive Officer, the highest-ranking executive in an organization responsible for making strategic decisions, managing operations, and leading the company towards its goals.

Change Management: The discipline of managing and guiding individuals, teams, and organizations through a process of transition or change.

Cloud Computing: The delivery of computing services over the internet, providing on-demand access to resources such as storage, processing power, and software.

Compliance: Adhering to regulations, standards, and guidelines related to health, safety, security, and quality in order to ensure legal and ethical practices.

Concept Development: The process of refining and developing an idea or concept, often in the early stages of product or project development.

COO: Chief Operating Officer, an executive responsible for the day-to-day operations and management of an organization.

Core production line: The central or essential processes and operations that drive a company's manufacturing.

Core Production Value Chain: The sequence of activities and processes involved in the creation, production, and delivery of the core product or service of a company. It represents the key steps that add value to the final product.

Corporate market segment: A specific group or segment of customers within the corporate or business-to-business (B2B) market.

Crypto Exchanges: Platforms where cryptocurrencies can be bought, sold, or exchanged for other digital assets or traditional currencies.

Culture: The shared values, beliefs, and behaviors within an organization or community.

Data Centers: Physical facilities that house computer systems and related components, such as servers and networking equipment.

Data Contextualization: The process of organizing and presenting data within a specific context or framework to derive meaningful insights.

Data Layers: The concept of organizing and structuring datasets by type, class, and nature to create a framework for navigating opportunities and use cases.

Data Management: The process of organizing, storing, securing, and maintaining data assets.

Data Modeling: The process of defining the structure, relationships, and attributes of data in a digital product or solution.

Data Ontologies: Standards and best practices for organizing and structuring data to enable better understanding, integration, and interoperability.

Data Platform: A software infrastructure that enables the storage, processing, and analysis of large volumes of data.

Data Strategy: A comprehensive plan that outlines how an organization collects, manages, analyzes, and utilizes data to support its business goals and objectives.

Data Taxonomies: Hierarchical classification systems used to organize and categorize data.

Data-driven: Guided by insights and decisions derived.

Dataset: A collection of related data elements or information that is organized and treated as a single unit.

Deep Learning: A subset of machine learning that uses artificial neural networks to learn and make predictions or decisions.

Digital Currency: A form of currency that exists only in electronic or digital form, typically decentralized and based on cryptographic technology (e.g., Bitcoin, digital yuan).

Digital Disruption: The transformation and upheaval caused by the introduction of new digital technologies and business models that significantly impact existing industries and markets.

Digital Maturity: The level of an organization's readiness and capability to effectively leverage digital technologies and approaches to drive innovation and business value.

Digital Product Management: The practice of overseeing the strategy, development, and management of digital products and services to meet customer needs and achieve business objectives.

Digital Product Manager: A professional responsible for the strategy, development, and management of digital products, often involving software or technology solutions.

Digital Transformation: The process of using digital technologies to drive significant changes in business operations, strategies, and customer experiences, with the goal of achieving enhanced performance and competitive advantage.

Digital Twin: A digital representation or replica of a physical entity, such as a product, process, or system, that allows for analysis, simulation, and optimization.

Digital Use Cases: Use cases that involve the application of digital technologies, analytics, or models to solve problems or achieve specific objectives.

Digitalization: The process of incorporating digital technologies and tools into various aspects of an organization or business to improve efficiency, effectiveness, and innovation.

Digitization: The process of transforming analog or manual processes into digital formats or utilizing digital technology.

Disruptive innovation: A type of innovation that creates significant shifts in markets, industries, or existing products and services.

Disruptive Technology: Technology that significantly alters the way businesses or industries operate.

Domain expertise: In-depth knowledge and understanding of a specific industry, field, or subject matter.

Downstream: Referring to activities or processes that occur later in the value chain, closer to the distribution and customer delivery stages.

Dynamic Data: Operational or time-varying datasets that capture information about changing conditions, measurements, or variables.

Ecosystem: A complex network or interconnected system of organizations, individuals, and technologies.

Embedded Domain Expertise: Incorporating specialized knowledge and expertise into digital systems or components.

Empirical method: A systematic approach to knowledge acquisition and problem-solving based on observation, experimentation, and evidence.

Enriched Digital Twin: A digital twin that incorporates additional data and information beyond the visual representation, such as operational data, sensor readings, or real-time information.

ERP (Enterprise Resource Planning): Integrated software systems that help organizations manage various aspects of their business operations.

E-wallets: Electronic wallets or digital wallets that allow users to store, manage, and make digital transactions with their money or assets.

Execution/Operations: The implementation and day-to-day activities necessary to execute a strategy or tactical plan.

External Datasets: Data from sources outside the immediate organization or system, which can be used to augment or enrich the existing data layers.

Fidelity of datasets: The accuracy, completeness, and reliability of the data.

Fintech: The application of technology and innovation to financial services and systems.

First-Generation Companies: Young startups that primarily focus on product development and sales functions, aiming to establish themselves in the market and survive the initial months or years of operation.

Frameworks: Structured models that provide guidance, principles, or best practices for decision-making or problem-solving.

Gap Analysis: The process of comparing the current state (AS-IS) and the desired state (TO-BE) to identify gaps or differences that need to be addressed.

Governance: The framework, policies, and processes for decision-making, control, and accountability within an organization.

Historical Data: Datasets that contain past records, events, or measurements, providing a historical perspective for analysis and decision-making.

Horizontal Scalability: The ability to scale a system by adding more instances or replicas horizontally, typically by distributing the workload across multiple machines or servers.

HSSQ: Health, Safety, Security, and Quality, which are critical aspects to consider and measure in industrial environments.

Human maturity: The growth, development, and maturation of individuals in terms of their cognitive, emotional, and behavioral capabilities.

Hybrid Cloud: A cloud computing environment that combines public and private cloud services.

Hyperbolic growth: Rapid and exponential expansion or development.

Hypothesis-driven Use Case Development: An approach where the development of use cases is guided by a clear hypothesis of the expected value creation.

Independent Cryptocurrencies: Decentralized digital currencies not issued or controlled by any government or central authority (e.g., Bitcoin).

Infrastructure-as-a-Service (IaaS): A cloud computing service model where organizations rent virtualized computing resources such as servers, storage, and networking.

Innovation: The process of introducing new ideas, methods, or products to create value and solve problems.

Insight-Driven Market: A market where the value and competitiveness of products or services are derived from their ability to provide meaningful insights to users.

Interconnectivity: The state of being connected or interconnected, often referring to the interconnectedness of digital technologies or systems.

Internal Services: Functions and processes within an organization that support its operations and employees.

IoT (Internet of Things): The network of interconnected physical devices and objects that can collect and exchange data.

Key Performance Indicators (KPIs): Quantifiable metrics used to measure and evaluate the performance and success of an organization or specific initiatives. KPIs provide insights into progress, effectiveness, and efficiency in achieving objectives.

Lean and agile organizations: Companies that prioritize efficiency, flexibility, and responsiveness to changes in the market.

Lean project: A project or initiative focused on eliminating waste, improving efficiency, and optimizing processes based on the principles of Lean management.

Machine Learning: A subset of artificial intelligence that enables systems to automatically learn and improve from experience without explicit programming.

Market Disruption: Significant changes or disturbances in a market or industry, often caused by the introduction of new technologies, products, or business models.

Market share: The portion or percentage of a market that a company or product controls or occupies.

Master Data: High-quality, consistent, and reliable data that serves as a single reference point for critical business information.

Maturity analysis: An assessment or evaluation of the level of maturity or development in a specific area, such as organizational culture or processes.

Metadata: Data that provides information about other data, describing the properties, attributes, or characteristics of the entities in a dataset.

Multi-Cloud: The use of multiple cloud service providers to meet different business needs or optimize resources.

National Digital Currency: A digital currency issued by a specific country's government or central bank.

Online Payment Solutions: Digital platforms or services that enable online transactions and payment processing.

Open APIs: Application Programming Interfaces that allow different software systems to interact and share data.

Optimization: The process of maximizing efficiency, performance, or effectiveness in a system or process, often through iterative improvements or fine-tuning.

Paradigm shift: A fundamental change in the way something is perceived, understood, or approached.

Parameters: Factors or variables that define or influence the behavior or outcome of a system or process.

Performance Levels: The speed, efficiency, and reliability at which a service or system operates.

Personality frameworks: Models or theories that categorize and describe different aspects of an individual's personality.

Platform-as-a-Service (PaaS): A cloud computing service model where organizations can develop, run, and manage applications without the complexity of building and maintaining the underlying infrastructure.

Predictive Maintenance: A maintenance strategy that uses data and analytics to predict and prevent equipment failures or breakdowns before they occur.

Principles: Fundamental truths or guidelines that serve as a foundation for decision-making and actions.

Private Cloud: A cloud computing environment dedicated to a single organization.

Problem Statement: A clear and concise description of the issue or challenge that the use case aims to solve.

Process Improvement: Enhancements made to the execution of tasks or operations to achieve greater efficiency, cost savings, or improved outcomes.

Process maturity: The level of effectiveness, efficiency, and control achieved in an organizational process over time.

Product development: The process of creating, designing, and bringing a new product to the market.

Product Improvement: Changes or enhancements made to the core product to enhance its quality, features, or attributes.

Production line: A sequence of operations or processes in a manufacturing environment that transforms raw materials into finished products.

Production Optimization: The focus on improving the efficiency and effectiveness of the production process to maximize output while maintaining quality. It includes minimizing waste, reducing production time, and optimizing resource utilization.

Project management: The discipline of planning, organizing, and managing resources to successfully complete projects within specific constraints of time, cost, and quality.

Proprietary Cloud: A cloud computing environment owned and operated by a specific organization.

Psychology of change: The study of human behaviors, attitudes, and emotions related to the process of change and innovation.

Public Cloud: A cloud computing environment shared among multiple organizations or users.

Qualitative Parameters: Non-numerical measures or attributes used to assess and describe the value created by the use case.

Quantitative Parameters: Numerical measures or metrics used to evaluate and quantify the value created by the use case.

Regulatory Bodies: Organizations responsible for creating and enforcing regulations and standards within a particular industry or sector.

Replicability: The possibility of reapplying a use case in the same or similar scenarios multiple times.

Resistance to change: The natural tendency of individuals to resist or be reluctant towards adopting or accepting new ideas, technologies, or processes.

RPA (Robotic Process Automation): The use of software robots or bots to automate repetitive and rule-based tasks or processes.

Scientific method: A systematic approach used in scientific research to formulate hypotheses, conduct experiments, gather data, and draw conclusions based on evidence.

Second-Generation Companies: Companies that have progressed beyond the startup phase and start to consolidate their operations by expanding the number of employees and developing supportive functions such as HR, finance, and service management while still focusing on sales and product development.

Serial number: An identification number assigned to a specific piece of equipment or product, providing a unique identifier for tracking and traceability purposes.

Software asset life cycle management: The process of managing and optimizing the lifecycle of software assets, including licensing, contracts, and procurement.

Software-as-a-Service (SaaS): A cloud computing service model where software applications are provided over the internet on a subscription basis.

Solution Design: The process of creating a plan or framework for solving a specific problem or achieving a desired outcome.

Sovereign Digital Currency: A digital currency issued and controlled by a government or central bank.

Spearheading: Introducing new concepts or ideas into large organizations by identifying departments or teams that are more open to change.

Staff Functions: Functions or departments in an organization that provide support and services to the core production or operational activities, such as HR, accounting, and legal departments.

Strategy: A plan of action or approach designed to achieve long-term goals and objectives.

Supply chain: The network of organizations, resources, activities, and processes involved in the creation and distribution of a product or service.

Tactics: Specific actions or methods employed to achieve a shorter-term goal or objective within the overall strategy.

Third-Generation Companies: Established, older, and larger organizations that may have a well-known brand and a trusted client base. They tend to focus on maintaining their market share with existing products rather than innovating for a changing market.

Top-down governance structure: A hierarchical approach to governance where decisions and policies are made at higher levels and cascaded down to lower levels of the organization.

Traditional Financial Institutions: Established banks, financial organizations, and institutions that operate using traditional banking practices.

Transformation initiatives: Projects or activities aimed at bringing significant changes or improvements to a company's operations, processes, or technologies.

Triangle of Possibility: A conceptual framework that represents the relationship between three parameters: finance, quality, and efficiency. Changes in one parameter can impact the other two.

Upstream: Referring to activities or processes that occur earlier in the value chain, closer to the raw materials or initial production stages.

Use Case: A specific example or scenario that describes how a product or service is used to address a particular problem or meet a specific need.

Value chain: The series of activities and processes involved in delivering a product or service to the end customer.

Value Stream Breakdown: The analysis and breakdown of the different areas of effect or value creation within the use case, which can be measured in various currencies (financial or non-financial).

Virtual Product: A product that exists in a digital or virtual form, such as digital friendships or online content.